Don't Worry Be Happy

9 Principles of Leading a Successful Life

JANE JOHN-NWANKWO RN, MSN, PHN

Don't Worry Be Happy
9 Principles of Leading a Successful Life

ISBN-13: 978-1516933730

ISBN-10: 1516933737

Printed in the United States of America

www.janejohn-nwankwo.com
www.djngbooks.org
www.janejohn-nwankwo.org

www.janejohn-nwankwo.com

www.djngbooks.org

www.janejohn-nwankwo.org

"Rejoice in the Lord always, and again I say Rejoice."

– Phillipians 4:4

OTHER TITLES FROM THE SAME AUTHOR:

Never Be Intimidated
A Motivational Book For Success

Weight Loss Inspiration

How To Start Your Own Business
The First 5 Steps

Nurses' Romance
Laurie & Andrew

Nurse Romance
Craig's Love Story

Hightime You Made a Move!
An inspirational & motivational book

SUCCESS IS FOR THE READY
A Motivational Book For Success

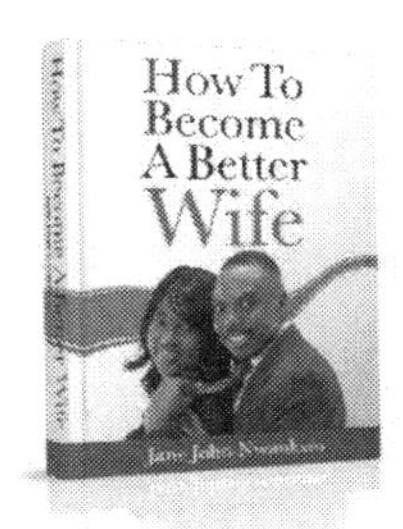
How To Become A Better Wife

PERSONALITY TYPES

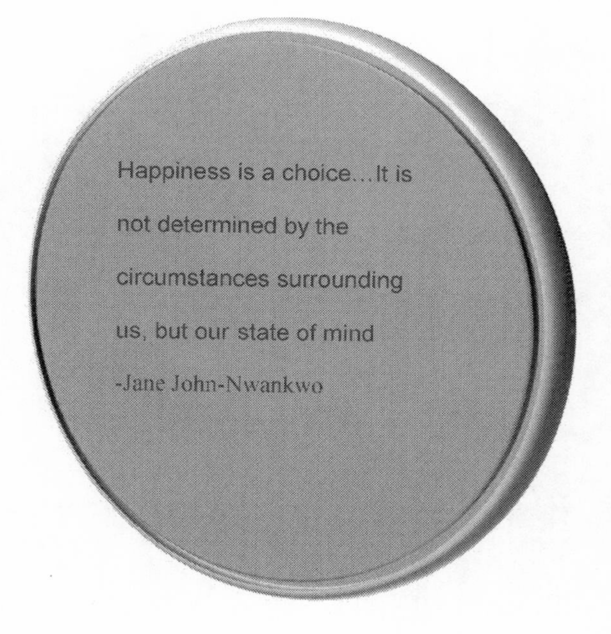
Happiness is a choice…It is
not determined by the
circumstances surrounding
us, but our state of mind
-Jane John-Nwankwo

Table of Contents

Prologue

Henry Ford once commented, "Coming together is a beginning; keeping together is progress; working together is success."

Success is such a subjective thing. If you were to ask twenty people to define success you would get as many radically different ideas. Some might say that success is having everything you need. Others may say it is being at the top of your field. Still others might define success in terms of income or conspicuous wealth. The philosophers might say success means being high on Maslow's Hierarchy of Needs.

It might be argued that success is a measure of one's perception. Those who are self-confident and have high self-esteem also feel successful where those with lower self-esteem often feel a lack of success.

Don't Worry Be Happy: 9 Strategies for Leading a Successful Life is about learning how to be successful, while maintaining a high level of optimism, peace of mind and faith in God.

Sometimes success is simply a matter setting a goal, devising a plan for achieving that goal and carrying out that plan. Each chapter of this book discusses a strategy that will help you achieve what you set out to do.

Coach Vince Lombardi told his team: "The price of success is hard work, dedication to the job at hand, and the determination that whether we win or lose, we have applied the best of ourselves to the task at hand."

Let us begin…..

Chapter One:
Approach Life with Optimism and Industry

Optimism is faith that leads to achievement. Nothing can be done without hope or confidence. ... No pessimist ever discovered the secret of the stars, or sailed to unchartered land, or opened a new doorway for the human spirit.

~Helen keller

Do you see the glass as half full or half empty? Your perception or outlook on life determines the degree of success you will achieve in everything you set out to do.

An optimistic outlook on life is absolutely vital to succeeding in everything you do. One of the landmark qualities of optimists is their happiness with their lives. Optimists are grateful for what life has given them. The song "Look on the Sunny Side" might have been written about optimists. They have a high level of happiness and satisfaction with their lives.

How optimistic are you? Optimism is key to bouncing back from adversity with high hopes for the future. It's sort of: "When the going gets tough, the tough see better times ahead."

SUCCESS IS PEACE OF MIND; PEACE OF MIND DESPITE YOUR HEALTH SITUATION, DESPITE YOUR FINANCIAL SITUATION, DESPITE CIRCUMSTANCES AROUND YOU -THAT IS SUCCESS.

Think about how you would react to these scenarios:

Your company is laying off staff. You are one of them. Do you:

- ✓ Feel sorry for yourself?
- ✓ Get angry at the company?
- ✓ Go into deep depression, convinced you will never find work?
- ✓ Use this opportunity to look for an equally satisfying job?

You're invited to a neighbour's party where you—new to the area—know no one. Do you?

- ✓ Stay home convinced you will be uncomfortable?
- ✓ See this as a great chance to get to know your neighbours?
- ✓ Hesitate because you are too shy to put yourself out there?
- ✓ Decide the entire thing will be a big bore?
- ✓ Pretend you didn't hear about or forgot about the invitation?

How you react to life's situations has a lot to do with your outlook on life. Optimism has wonderful powers. It can cure or prevent depression. Optimism can even fight off colds and heart attacks. This morning, we had a power outage, which means nothing is working at the office, the phones cannot ring, internet cannot work, I had a class to teach but we needed to make copies for the students, the class consists of many videos which cannot be shown because there was no power. As I talked with my administrative assistant who was really concerned, I told her 'Let us take it one minute at a time'. "One minute at a time?" she asked with laughter, " I said "Yes, one minute at a time, not one day at a time". I was calmly figuring out how to restructure the class to still make it a success. Luckily, within a short while, the lights were back on. We laughed it off "The minutes worked, LOL" I texted her.

You can learn to make simple changes in your thinking patterns to become more positive. Becoming more positive will aid in your quest to lead a successful life. Optimists believe, "It can happen to me." Then they set out to achieve it—confident they have what it takes to succeed.

Optimism is one of the elements of our emotional intelligence quotient. Emotional intelligence is the ability to identify and manage our own emotions and to recognize the emotions of others. It is a communication path between the rational and emotive sides of our brain. There is a direct link between our level of optimism and our happiness. Our EQ is a predictor of personal and professional success.

Optimists have been found to have a high level of energy. They are industrious, hard-working, creative, inspired, empowered, grateful, self-confident, and productive. Optimists are physically and emotionally healthy. They see possibilities and are "big picture thinkers". Optimists have successful careers, better educational qualifications. They are better at building relationships and solving problems. Optimists are more resilient in the face of adversity and cope

EMOTIONAL INTELLIGENCE IS THE ABILITY TO RECOGNIZE AND MANAGE OUR EMOTIONS AND TO RECOGNIZE THE EMOTIONS OF OTHERS.

better with failure. They see failures as "temporary setbacks" and "learning opportunities".

There are some disadvantages of being an optimist. It's often hard to remain positive in the face of negative and pessimistic people. Pessimists find optimists unrealistic and sometimes downright irritating. But the advantages of optimism far outweigh the disadvantages.

There are ways to stay optimistic in the face of challenging situations:

Make a list of the positives in scenarios. Identify best and worst case.

When you know what you are up against, it helps you plan for any contingency. Looking at the worst case scenario allows you to brace for the direst of circumstances. It helps you become resilient. Looking at the best case scenario should never include unrealistic long shots. For example: the scenarios considered should provide an accurate picture of the outcomes. A "good" scenario should not include winning the lottery. While it is a wonderful dream it is hardly feasible. Improbable, unrealistic scenarios are not useful.

See the humor in life. Smile and laugh every day.

Unfortunately, in this serious business of living, many of us have forgotten the value of humor. Humor can make us more resilient in times of stress, sadness and crisis. Humor can help us deal with change and uncertainty.

How much happier and more successful people are when they face life with a smile, with laughter, and joy.

Laurence Peter said, "Realize that a sense of humor is deeper than laughter and more satisfying than comedy and delivers more rewards than merely being entertaining. A sense of humor sees the fun in everyday experiences. It is more important to have fun than it is to be funny."

Build laughter into your day. Always be ready to invite humor into your life. Great humor connects to our shared funny experiences both at home and at work. Laugh not at others but with them. Always be on the lookout for the funny things in life.

Humor is infectious. When you hear others laughing you want to laugh too. Shared laughter binds people together and increases happiness, camaraderie and success. Laughter triggers healthy physical changes. Laughter strengthens your immune system, boosts your energy, diminishes pain, and protects you from the stress. Laughter is fun, free, and easy to use and it can make a huge difference in your life. Dr. Paul McGhee says, "Your sense of humor is one of the most powerful tools you have to make certain that your daily mood and emotional state support good health."

ALWAYS SEE THE FUNNY THINGS IN EVERYDAY LIFE. REMEMBER THAT HAVING FUN IN LIFE IS MORE THAN BEING FUNNY. FUNNY PEOPLE MAY NOT REALLY BE HAVING FUN. EVEN IN YOUR SERIOUS WORK PLACE, FIND LITTLE THINGS TO MAKE YOU LAUGH

Surround yourself with others who are positive. Both positivity and negativity are contagious.

Model Heidi Klum advises: "I think it's important to get your surroundings as well as yourself into a positive state - meaning surround yourself with positive people, not the kind who are negative and jealous of everything you do."

Like humor, being positive is contagious. Sadly so, too, is negativism. If you surround yourself with people for whom the glass is always half empty and nothing is ever quite right, then they will drag down your mood and sap the energy you need to be successful. Instead, choose to be in the company of optimists who will buoy your spirits. A positive outlook is so important when you are reaching for goals. Positive people give you the confidence you need to persevere.

If you put yourself in a positive frame of mind, you can accomplish just about anything you set your mind to. A positive attitude helps you see your goals clearly and feel as if they are within your grasp. When you surround yourself with positive people, positive images and positive visualizations, it is amazing what you can do.

Express gratitude every day.

Gratitude is a powerful emotion. It can make us feel happier. A five-minute a day gratitude journal has been proven to increase your long-term happiness by more than 10 percent. This is the same effect as doubling your income!

Gratitude makes us more likable and trustworthy. Those who express gratitude are deemed nicer, more social, and more appreciative than those who do not express gratitude. People who express gratitude make more friends, deepen existing friendships, and improve their marriages. When you recognize that someone went out their way to do something for and you say it out in their presence, it makes both of you –the 'thanker' and the 'thankee'happy.

Gratitude makes us healthier. Studies have shown that people who express gratitude spend 20% more time exercising, report 15% less pain, have 16% fewer physical symptoms of poor health and improve sleep by over 25%. Keeping a gratitude journal decreased depression symptoms by 35% in only a few weeks. Patients who were told to make at least one entry a week showed a significantly improved blood pressure.

Gratitude makes us more successful in our careers. It has been shown to make managers more effective. Gratitude improves networking, decision making and productivity. Gratitude makes mentors and coaches more effective. Gratitude helps you achieve your career goals. Gratitude make a friendlier, more enjoyable workplace.

Gratitude strengthens emotions. It banishes envy and stress. Gratitude makes us more optimistic, happier and healthier. Gratitude has been shown to increase lifespan in years.

Grateful people are less materialistic. Materialism is strongly correlated with a lower self-concept, greater self-centeredness, and a lack of confidence and higher levels of depression. Those who put a high value on things are frequently unhappy and dissatisfied. People who want more feel less competent. Feelings of relatedness and gratitude increase our ability to appreciate and enjoy the good in life.

Gratitude makes us think outside ourselves. We become more spiritual and less self-centred. By its very nature, gratitude shifts our focus on others. Gratitude is a powerful form of self-esteem therapy. It focuses the individual back on himself. When you see how important people are, you indirectly see how important you are yourself.

Gratitude makes you more resilient to life's problems and challenges. Those that have more gratitude have a pro-active coping style. They are more likely to have a social support system on which they rely in times of need. They deal better with things like stress and PTSD.

If you are having problems with sleep, try writing in your gratitude journal before you go to bed. Gratitude increases sleep quality. It reduces the time required to fall asleep. It increases sleep duration. It is believed this is because of the frame of mind you are in when you fall asleep. Gratitude helps us relax and eases stress. Positive emotions like gratitude are among the strongest relaxants.

GRATITUDE IS A POWERFUL SELF-ESTEEM THERAPY. THE MORE YOU REALIZE HOW IMPORTANT PEOPLE ARE, THE YOU REALIZE HOW IMPORTANT YOU ARE YOURSELF

Expect highs and lows in life and learn to roll with the punches.

As Anna Paquin notes: "I think it is an amazing quality to be able to roll with the punches and not be totally ruined as a person because life is rough for you. That's a really admirable way to go through life."

When you can accept setbacks, obstacles, and hurdles on your way to reaching your goal, you are resilient. This is a valuable quality because life won't always be smooth sailing.

On the other hand, life sometimes offers you shortcuts and quick solutions but you don't want to grow accustomed to things falling naturally into place because that's not realistic either. You need to be prepared for "Murphy 's Law". Anything that can go wrong probably will. But, at the same time you need to recognize that sometimes things will go well too and that either way you've got what it takes to continue towards your goal.

Having a support system—friends, colleagues, family—is a help in dealing with the tough times and keeping you optimistic. Do not be ashamed to ask for help. I was teaching a continuous education class yesterday and one of my nurse assistant students taught us another good lesson about asking for help. She had been working as a night shift nurse assistant and had continually been assigned 24 patients every night she worked. She continued to do it for three years until she had a nerve damage in her arm related to constant turning of patients.

It was during the investigation that she realized that she had been overworking for 3 years. Each nurse assistant is supposed to have not more than 12 patients. So, she has been taking 2 people's loads for 3 years. Even though, she felt overwhelmed, she never asked for help because she thought everyone had 24 patients.

See mistakes not as bad things but as learning opportunities.

We live in a time when precision is praised and mistakes are often a cause of shame. Mistakes should be viewed instead as learning opportunities. What went wrong? How can we fix it? What did we learn from this situation?

Remember: out of mistakes came great inventions like Post It Notes, penicillin, the Slinky, Silly Putty, chocolate chip cookies, potato chips, the Pacemaker, microwave ovens, artificial sweetener, fireworks, Scotchguard, Corn Flakes, x-rays and ink jet printers. If you risk trying new things you are bound to make mistakes. Trial and error are part of the learning process.

President Clinton said, "If you live long enough, you'll make mistakes. But if you learn from them, you'll be a better person. It's how you handle adversity, not how it affects you. The main thing is never quit, never quit, never quit."

Mistakes should never be a reason to give up but rather incentive to try another avenue. Engineer John Hopps was conducting research on hypothermia. During his experiment he realized that if a heart stopped beating due to cooling it could be restarted by artificial stimulation. This veering in a different direction away from his original study was the birth of the pacemaker.

Frustrated with his search for a "wonder drug" that would cure diseases Dr. Alexander Fleming threw out his "mistakes". Then he noticed a mold had formed in one of the Petri dishes. That mold was the birth of penicillin. Had Dr. Fleming given up, thousands of people would have died from diseases penicillin has cured.

Set your goals high but don't get caught up in perfectionism.

Trying to do things perfectly is commendable. However, there are times and there are limits. Often too much time is wasted and perfectly good products and solutions scrapped because they were not perfect. In reality, very good is often quite sufficient.

In chapter one of my book, *It's In Your Hands: 5 Strategies to Achieving Your Life Dreams*, I wrote about how perfection is related to procrastination. Procrastinators tend to be perfectionists. They avoid tasks because they are insecure. They feel they must be perfect to please others. So they often put things off and then fret that they won't be loved unless what they do is perfect.

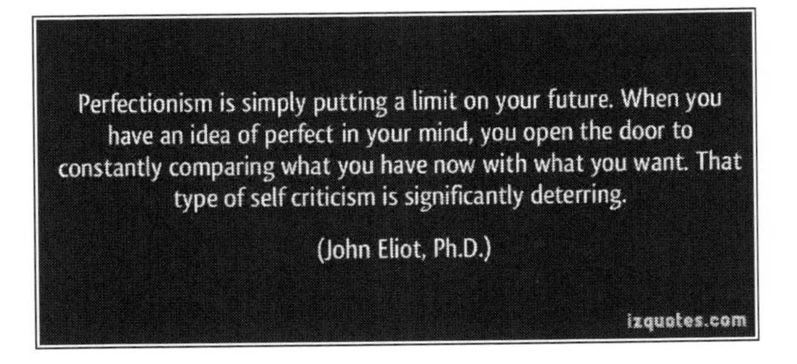

Photo courtesy of izquotes.com

Focus on your strengths and talents and make them work to your advantage.

If you play piano badly but you are a good cook, it is only sensible that you look for success in your area of strength. As much as I would have loved to be an operating room nurse, I knew it was not for me because each time I inhaled a good amount of the odour of blood, I saw myself blacking out. My problem is not the sight of blood, After all I have been teaching Blood withdrawal classes practically every month since 2009 and we draw tubes and tubes of blood each time. Since the blood are in tubes, and I don't inhale the odor, I have no problem. I had to accept that there was something in the smell or odour of blood that my system would not just accept. Instead of feeling bad, that I could not be an operating room nurse, I capitalized on my other strengths, and believe me, my strengths are numerous. Do not dwell on your weaknesses, instead, capitalize on your strength, do the things you love and be happy.

We are always happier doing something we like and are good at. Of course, perfectionism has its benefits, especially in work, where it motivates over-achievers to strive for high standards and new dreams. Perfectionists are driven to improve and innovate. They are extremely self-disciplined and detail-oriented. These qualities are critical professions like surgery, marksmanship, war strategies, and air traffic control. There is no margin for error, but think less of being a perfectionist, or you will achieve less in life. As a single lady, I loved my apartment to be sparkling clean. In fact, my husband- then friend commented that the first day he came into my apartment with his friend, as they were leaving, they were arguing over who should ask me out because I was too clean and organized.

Many years later with three restless children, I look at my house, remember how perfectly clean and organized I used to be, and I smile at the futility of perfectionism. After trying to clean and reorganize things every minute, and realizing I was working myself to death, I had to let go and accept the fact that this was not just my home anymore, but the home of five human beings, and that is when I found my joy. Let kids be kids, schedule clean-up times, and let everybody be happy.

However, there is another side to this coin and that's the old adage: "Until someone put skates on Eric Heiden, no one knew he could skate." See my book *Personality Types.*

If we spend our time and energy honing identified skills and talents who knows how many athletes, musicians, researchers and world leaders would never have emerged. It is important to develop talents and strengths. But, it is also important to try new things.

The problem with perfectionism arises when it is taken to extremes. Perfectionists set standards for themselves and others that are simply impossible to meet. Then because it isn't perfect, they devalue work that was useful and practical. Self-directed perfectionism can lead to obsessiveness, inefficiency, and serious mental health issues. These can affect attendance, performance, and morale. Perfectionists often procrastinate. They are paralyzed by fear of failing before they begin.

As Sivakumar Palaiappan points out: "I sincerely believe in 'Play to your strengths' One could become mediocre when he/she focus on weakness, but focusing on strengths only can take people to excellence."

Rogier van der Maas makes this point well when he says, "...you should always focus on your strengths, but I also think you should not forget about your weaknesses...Spend your time wisely, but don't fall for that easy way out by saying: hey, it's not my strength…[and] shirk and delegate to others." You might very well have been the best person for that job—if you had been prepared to take a risk.

Optimism is the key to leading a successful life. Without optimism, it is hard to recover from failure. Optimism gives us the strength to bounce back and try again when things don't go as planned. Seeing things optimistically also gives us time and belief to help others. It helps us be grateful for what we have. When we understand how lucky we are, we can offer to help those who are less fortunate.

The creed of Optimist International has some solid advice about how to use optimism as a tool for a successful life. It states,

> *Promise yourself…to be just as enthusiastic about the success of others as you are about your own.*
> *To forget the mistakes of the past and press on to the greater achievements of the future.*
> *To wear a cheerful countenance at all times and give every living creature you meet a smile.*
> *To give so much time to the improvement of yourself that you have no time to criticize others.*

To be too large for worry, too noble for anger, too strong for fear, and too happy to permit the presence of trouble.

These are optimistic words by which we could all live. Success is measured by how happy and satisfied we feel with our life. As Charles Spurgeon pointed out, “It’s not how much we have but how much we enjoy that makes happiness.”

Helpful Resources

Ang, J. “Does Being Optimistic at Work Really Help?” http://www.humanresourcesonline.net/optimistic-work-really-help/

Beattie, L. “Optimism and the Power of Positive Thinking”. http://www.sparkpeople.com/resource/wellness_articles.asp?id=835

Blood, B. P. (2012) *Optimism: the Lesson of Ages.* http://www.chapters.indigo.ca/en-ca/books/product/9781272747855-item.html?mkwid=sglCNn6VL_dc&pcrid=44154474422&pkw=&pmt=&s_campaign=goo-Shopping_Books&gclid=CjwKEAjwwZmsBRDOh7C6rKO8zkcSJABCusnbgPx4q_Yw-EFYD7iQVCLu-78tov0zJ2T3JcskfwtcVBoCyEjw_wcB

Buckingham, M. and Clifton, D. *Now, Discover Your Strengths.* http://www.amazon.com/Discover-Your-Strengths-Marcus-Buckingham/dp/0743201140/

de Ridder, D. "The Relative Benefits of Being Optimistic" in *British Journal of Health Psychology.* http://onlinelibrary.wiley.com/doi/10.1348/135910700168829/abstract

Dewitt Hyde, W. (2009) The Art of Optimism as Taught by Robert Browning. http://www.chapters.indigo.ca/en-ca/books/product/9781113362308-item.html?mkwid=sglCNn6VL_dc&pcrid=44154474422&pkw=&pmt=&s_campaign=goo-Shopping_Books&gclid=CjwKEAjwwZmsBRDOh7C6rKO8zkcSJABCusnb0_8J4vW9ZN4T1Ig1Lnxvq9s3blNyq52Nk6A8PYFl1RoC9KLw_wcB

Diener, E. and Eunkook, M. (2003) *Culture and Subjective Well-Being.* http://www.amazon.com/Culture-Subjective-Well-Being-Being-Quality/dp/0262541467/ref=sr_1_2?s=books&ie=UTF8&qid=1423596529&sr=1-2

Dutton, J. (2014) How to be a Positive Leader. http://www.amazon.com/How-Be-Positive-Leader-Actions/dp/1626560285/ref=sr_1_1?ie=UTF8&qid=1423849208&sr=8-1&keywords=how%20to%20be%20a%20positive%20leader

Emmons, R. (2013) *Gratitude Works: A 21-Day Program for Creating Emotional Prosperity.* http://www.amazon.com/Gratitude-Works-Creating-Emotional-Prosperity/dp/1118131290/ref=sr_1_2?s=books&ie=UTF8&qid=1423597826&sr=1-2

Lopez, S. *Positive Psychology: Exploring the Best in People.* http://www.amazon.com/Positive-Psychology-volumes-Exploring-People/dp/0275993507/ref=sr_1_12?s=books&ie=UTF8&qid=1423599437&s

r=1-12&keywords=shane%20lopez

Lyubomirsky, S. and Kurtz, Jaime. (2013) *Positively Happy: Sustainable Happiness.* http://www.amazon.com/Positively-Happy-Sustainable-Happiness-Psychology/dp/1483918580/ref=sr_1_4?s=books&ie=UTF8&qid=1423600479&sr=1-4&keywords=Sonja%20Lyubomirsky

Pychyl, T. "Optimism and Perceived Competence: Resilience Resources" in *Psychology Today.* https://www.psychologytoday.com/blog/dont-delay/200903/optimism-and-perceived-competence-resilience-resources

Rath, T. *StrengthsFinder 2.0.* *http://www.amazon.com/StrengthsFinder-2-0-Tom-Rath/dp/159562015X*

Chapter Two:
Learn to See the Big Picture. Get Your Priorities Right

I dare you to think bigger, to act bigger, and to be bigger. I promise you a richer more exciting life if you do.
~William Danforth

A single thought — if cultivated — grows over time into the empowering habit of big picture thinking. This eventually takes over this person's psychology, and propels him towards the achieving his objectives. That's why big picture thinking is vital to leading a successful life.

Seeing the big picture means not getting so caught up in the details that you lose sight of where you are going. The Stonecutter's story exemplifies why it is important to be a "big picture" thinker.

Once upon a time there was a stonecutter. Every day he went into the mountains to cut stones from the rocks. While working, the stonecutter always sang merrily. He was happy with his life. He had plenty to eat and no worries.

One day, he had to drop a load of stones at a villa owned by a very wealthy man. When he saw the beautiful house, a crushing sadness descended upon him. For the first time in his life he yearned to be rich. He sighed. "Wouldn't I love to own this beautiful home and have loads of money," he said. "Then I wouldn't have to sweat to earn my keep."

The stonecutter was amazed to hear a voice say, "Your wish is granted. From now on you will get what you wish for."

Naturally, the stonecutter was shocked and skeptical.

Had he been dreaming?

When he arrived home that afternoon he saw a beautiful villa on the spot where his old hut had been.

Delighted, the now-wealthy stonecutter gave up working. He started to live the high life.

One muggy afternoon he looked out the window. The king drove by in his magnificent carriage.

Without thinking, the stonecutter said to himself, " I would love to be the king. Then I would ride about in that cool carriage."

Instantly, his wish was granted.

However, riding in that cool carriage was a lot hotter than he had expected.

He looked out the window, surprised by the intensity of the sun's rays. It was so hot that the sun seemed to be burning right through the carriage's thick walls.

"If I were the sun," he sighed. "I'd do things differently."

Once again his wish came true. He now sent waves of heat into the universe.

For a while he had no more wishes.

But one rainy day when he tried in vain to break through a thick blanket of cloud, the stonecutter wished to be a cloud with the power to stop the sun.

So he became a cloud. Then, he turned into rain. He fell on the earth and flowed down a hill. But, a massive boulder forced him to go a different way.

"What?" he raged. "Is a rock like this more powerful than I am? Fine! Then I wish to be a rock!"

Instantly, there he was, on the mountainside, being a rock. He hardly had time to rejoice about his new shape, when he suddenly heard a cracking sound coming from somewhere below. He looked down. To his great horror, he saw a stonecutter hacking pieces off him.

"What?! That man is stronger than I am?"

So he turned back into a stonecutter. Once more, he went into the mountains hewing stone, under the hot sun and in the pouring rain, always with a song on his lips. He was happy with what he had and what he was.

This story is not about being content with what you have, it is about viewing the bigger picture before you proceed. In business as in life, seeing the consequences of our decisions and how they affect the whole picture is important.

Seeing the big picture involves seeing how things connect and how one thing affects another. If you hope to succeed as an entrepreneur, you have to develop a feeling for who your stakeholders are and figure out how to make them all winners. Whenever you make a decision, it should be a positive one for your clients.

Some people are natural big picture thinkers. Others have to learn this skill. The direct opposite of a big picture person is a details thinker. This is not a right-wrong spectrum. There is a time and need for both. The big picture people tend to be creative, strategic, and visionary. The downside is that they can also be messy, disorganized, and forgetful.

Details thinkers get lost in the minutiae. They are often criticized for lacking common sense, failing to prioritize or overlooking cause-effect. For example, details people study well for multiple choice tests because they have a keen attention to detail and have a great memory for details. They do poorly on theme, main idea and essay questions because they miss the larger picture.

HAVING A GENERAL IDEA OF WHAT THE CONSEQUENCES OF YOUR DECISIONS WOULD BE IS A KEY PRINCIPLE OF BEING HAPPY

Details people are conscientious, exacting, and meticulous. They are planners. However, details persons can't see the forest for the trees. They lose—or lack—perspective. They cannot put things in priority.

Big picture thinkers and details people often complement each other. They work well together—or drive one another crazy!

Often a company CEO is a big picture person while the COO and the CFO are the details people. It's a natural match. Each has character traits which their job description requires.

Sometimes, it is not this simple in work or in life. The demands of work and home most likely demand both skills. Most people are naturally better at one than the other. A lucky few do both equally well. Whether you have good attention to detail or whether you can see the big picture easily and clearly is generally a big part of your personality. However big picture thinking can be learned and used when needed.

Big picture thinkers see complex patterns and cause-effect relationships. They are energized by new projects and new challenges. Big picture thinkers have a low tolerance for boring, repetitive tasks. They abhor busy work, paper reporting and filling out forms. They are great at seeing what needs to be done but fuzzy or unconcerned about the steps required to arrive there.

How to Become a Big Picture Thinker

1. Take time to think

We get so caught up in the demands of work of our lives that we seldom give ourselves time for thinking. You need to allow yourself time to percolate. If you go from one "must do" to the next you never get time to step back and consider the whole thing. Instead of dashing madly from one urgent task to another putting out fires, set aside a block of time each day when you are most creative for thinking. For ladies, if you enjoy cooking, you can leave your cell phone in the bedroom while cooking and use your cooking time to think. TV time can never be thinking time.

Married people reading this book will agree with me that many a time when you spend time talking things over with your spouse and thinking, you will discover how much you didn't think about in your busy day to day work. Taking time to think things over with no distractions at the time of thinking has helped my husband and I achieve a lot.

Enjoy Problem Solving

Big picture thinkers see a problem as a challenge waiting to be solved. They are energized by the prospect.

2. Discover the Benefits of Brainstorming

Thinking alone we often reach stumbling blocks. Great ideas often bubble up through brainstorming or talking about ideas with another person with whom you can share ideas and combine thoughts.

3. Select Specific Goals

This is where you sift through your big-picture thinking to arrive at a handful of specific goals. Next it is time to make these into actionable statements. For example if you want to renovate your house or redesign a product at work, break this down into more specific actions and establish a timeline: For example, I want to write a draft for the product roadmap over the next two years. Break this into specific steps: "By December 31, I will…" , I am trying to proof-read this book before the publishing, since the book is almost 200 pages, I am trying to proof-read 40 pages every day for the next 5 days.

Big picture questions are often broad and the task seems insurmountable.

Decompose the big picture question into smaller manageable pieces that feel doable. Identify a specific problem. Generate several solutions. The problem: Ineffective communication in the workplace. Solutions: Establish a mentorship process for sharing.

4. Make Bold Big Decisions

Big picture thinkers are not afraid to make a decision and are willing to go against the flow of conformity to do so.

5. Solution Oriented

Big picture thinking big is about finding solutions, answers and ideas that will break down the walls that are standing in your way of solving the problem. It involves asking effective questions that will expand the possibilities and open up alternative perspectives that we never considered before.

6. Take Calculated Risks

In order to solve problems, big picture thinkers are risk takers. But they do not jump in impetuously. They do their homework first.

7. Identify First Steps

Often a big picture idea doesn't get off the ground because no one defines what should happen first. If the goal is big, procrastination on tackling it often occurs. It is critical to choose the first steps. It might be as simple as doing a google search or inventorying what is already on hand or collecting documents related to the issue or forming a discussion group. If you don't know where you're going you will usually end up somewhere else.

8. Research

Before big picture thinkers reach a solution or arrive at a decision after they do the research. Big picture thinkers are efficient researchers, amassing the data, sifting through it,

analysing and synthesizing the information to reach a solution. In my many years in business, I have realized the importance of research. "My people perish for lack of knowledge…" (Hosea 4:6) applies not only to the knowledge of the word of God, but also to the knowledge of how to solve problems around us.

A simple example is when I needed to take a loan, because of my limited knowledge on the availability of loans for business, I took a choking loan with so much interest. After I had paid off that loan through my nose, I discovered an easier loan. I beat myself at how much I lost just because I did not do enough research.

BIG PICTURE THINKERS ARE NOT AFRAID TO MAKE DECISIONS BECAUSE THEY KNOW THAT ACHIEVING BIG GOALS INVOLVES MAKING ONE DECISION AT A TIME.

9. Be Forward Thinking

Big picture thinking demands forward thinking. Big picture thinkers are always several steps ahead, several moves in advance and many years into the future.

10. Step Outside Your Comfort Zone

Big picture thinkers are risk takers who can think outside the box. They use the following techniques:

Guided visualization: See yourself solving the problem.

Visioning: What will it look like when my goal is achieved?

Well Duh!: The answer was right there all along. How could I have missed this?

Council of Heroes: Imagine yourself sitting in a room with the great minds of all time solving this problem.

Clearing up Assumptions: What assumptions are you and your team implicitly making about the problem? Ask yourself: What would happen if this assumption was removed? Removing assumptions can free up your mind to see the bigger picture.

Bird's Eye View: Every team brings a unique perspective to the problem. How can your team's lens reshape the solution to this problem? What are the relevant ways in which your team thinks differently? How is it useful?

Get into the Habit of Thinking Big: Incorporate the habit of big picture thinking into every part of your life. Think big about:

- Daily tasks, routines, projects and goals.

- Your contributions to making the world better.
- Your ability to think creatively, outside the box.
- Your capacity for problem solving, critical thinking, analysis and synthesis.
- Your capacity to value others.
- Your ability to overcome obstacles and challenges.
- Your capacity to imagine the possibilities.
- Your life's purpose and aims.

11. Know Strengths and Talents

Big picture thinkers take into account their personal strengths, talents and abilities. The idea they conceptualize makes use of their strong attributes and talents. Make the most use of your talents, capitalize on your strengths and when you need to delegate, do not hesitate to do so.

12. **Motivation and Dedication**

Big picture thinkers are highly motivated to solve problems and achieve goals. They have a high degree of dedication to their cause. They will spare no effort to bring their ideas to fruition. They will only discuss their goals with individuals who have the same motivating spirit as they do.

13. **See Things from all Angles**

Big picture thinkers consistently reframe their problems. They expand the possibilities and perspectives, twisting their view of the problem in a creative way to help them brainstorm better ideas and solutions.

14. Unshakable Belief

Because you have sifted the assumptions, and have given enough time to thinking, big picture thinking involves unwavering belief in yourself and your ideas. When I started my business, I did not make a dime for 12 months, I used my hard earned night shift nursing pay checks to fund my business, but I kept going because I knew what lay ahead. When the money finally started coming, it has never stopped. Glory to God for keeping my spirit up in the very discouraging start-up times.

15. Surround themselves with Other Big Picture Thinkers

Big picture thinkers associate with other big picture thinkers. They thrive on the ambitions, motivation and inspiration of others to think bigger than they ever imagined possible.

Things that Impede Big-Picture Thinking

Inflexibility: “We've always done it this way.” Inflexible thinking is like wearing blinders. You see only a part of the whole picture and refuse to consider other alternatives to the status quo.

Limiting Ideas: “It won't work.” Yes trying new things is messy and it might not work but how will you know unless you take a risk and try it?

Lack of Self Confidence: “I can't do it.” You won't know until you try. Unless the attempt is life threatening or financially disastrous what's the real harm? If you succeed others will be encouraged to try new things and your self-confidence will receive a boost.

Conformity: "People will think I am nuts!" President John F. Kennedy noted: Conformity is the jailer of freedom and the enemy of growth." Without people to buck the system where would we be today? Non-comformists like Rosa Parks, Nelson Mandela, Dr. Martin Luther King, Junior, Walt Disney weren't afraid of what people would say or think about their ideas.

Bette Midler identifies a problem in conformity: Group conformity scares the pants off me because it's so often a prelude to cruelty towards anyone who doesn't want to - or can't - join the Big Parade.

Procrastination:

"I'll get around to it someday." Transfixed by fear of failure, perfectionists delay things. Those lacking self-confidence are afraid they won't be up to the task. Consequently procrastinators derail projects, disappoint their bosses and irritate their co-workers who need that piece of the puzzle.

Short-sighted thinking:

"I don't know how to get it started."

In his book, Long-Term Thinking for a Short-Sighted World, Jim Brumm states: "In today's world we are grappling at every turn with an increasing energy shortage, food production systems that struggle to feed increasing millions, environmental problems that threaten our survival, a debt crisis that is crippling individuals and governments, and so much more.

All of these problems come with their own unique challenges and examined on their own they may seem completely different from each other, but they share one common, rarely discussed hidden thread that runs through the center of each and binds them together: a lack of long-term thinking. We're very bad long-term thinkers."

Negative thinking:

"It'll never fly Orville." If Orville Wright and thousands of other inventors had given up because others were pessimists, we would have been deprived of all sorts of things we take for granted like electricity, airplanes, pacemakers, open heart surgery, and cochlear implants.

Negative thinking is an obstacle to improvement. Any change feels impossible. Negative thinkers can't see the small steps to reaching a big ending.

Negative thinkers lack the energy and motivation to take big steps. They feel stuck. They cannot envision that in order to "eat the elephant" you do it one spoonful at a time.

Excuses:

"I don't have the materials." You can always make excuses to avoid doing something.

George Washington Carver observed: Ninety-nine percent of the failures come from people who have the habit of making excuses.

It is easy to make excuses as a crutch. Carlos Santana pointed out that excuses are a great deflect for not changing destructive habits: "Most people don't have that willingness to break bad habits. They have a lot of excuses and they talk like victims."

Details-thinking:

"I have to complete these urgent tasks first." Details are like excuses. They will always give you license for not getting started.

Details thinking is necessary in devising an action plan for your goals. Without these steps, the goals will never be achieved.

However, you can get so caught up in minute details that no action ever occurs.

Over analysis:

"I have to map out a plan before I begin."

Like details thinking over-analysing stalls action and nothing productive gets done. Author Rebecca Jane said, "Over analysis leads to paralysis."

Perfectionism:

"This has to be perfect. What if I make a mistake?"

Perfectionists procrastinate because they are afraid of making mistakes. They waste time and throw out products and ideas which would have been just fine because in their minds, the idea or plan or product wasn't perfect.

Perfectionists are hard on themselves and others who must live or work with them. Martha Stewart and Steve Jobs have been criticized for being too perfectionistic.

Arianna Huffington advises parents, "The fastest way to break the cycle of perfectionism and become a fearless mother is to give up the idea of doing it perfectly - indeed to embrace uncertainty and imperfection."

Fear:

"I'm afraid to try something unorthodox." It is a scary thing to go upstream against the tide of conformity. You might be judged harshly. You might fail and make a fool of yourself. But nothing new ever evolved from conformity. The risk takers of the world made all the startling breakthroughs. As musician and bandleader Les Brown pointed out, "Too many of us are not living our dreams because we are living our fears."

No Incentive:

"Why should I risk my job/reputation/social standing to try something unproven?"

We live in a results-oriented society. If there isn't a prize, a promotion, or money involved many people are reluctant to expend energy on something.

But as Mohammed Yunus notes, every incentive should not be tangible. He states, "Making money is a happiness. And that's a great incentive. Making other people happy is a super-happiness."

In our concrete, results-oriented thinking we often overlook the great intangible rewards involved in doing things for others.

Seeing the big picture is about making grand goals, big dreams and high hopes that people aspire to in every stage an aspect of their lives. How can you grasp and retain the Big Picture? What does it take?

Getting Your Priorities Correct

Getting your priorities right is all about making intelligent choices. It involves deciding which goals to pursue and in which order to pursue them. It requires vision and foresight. Intelligent people rise over today's obstructions and gaze over the hills and the valleys of the future. They see the invisible and the challenges it presents. Legendary entrepreneurs like: Bill Gates, Steve Jobs, and Mark Zuckerberg possess such vision and foresight that they were able to see how technology could change the lives of us all. Then they created products and services that will turn their vision into reality.

Before we can get our priorities straight we need to know what our priorities actually are. How do we set priorities?

Helpful Resources

Babauta, L. "Setting Priorities" in *Success Magazine*. http://www.success.com/article/setting-priorities

Brumm, J. (2012) Long-Term Thinking for a Short-Sighted World: Restoring Happiness, Balance, and Sanity to Ourselves and Our Planet"http://www.amazon.com/Long-Term-Thinking-Short-Sighted-World-Restoring/dp/1612641245

Collucci, A. (2011) Big Picture Thinking. http://www.amazon.com/Aileen-Zeitz-Collucci-Picture-Thinking/dp/B005O87ISA

Cope, K. (2012) *Seeing the Big Picture*. http://www.amazon.ca/Seeing-Big-Picture-Business-Credibility/dp/1608322467

Ideas into Action. "Aligning Resources with Priorities: Focusing on what Matters Most". http://www.edu.gov.on.ca/eng/policyfunding/leadership/IdeasIntoAction12.pdf

Nelson, J. and Bolles, R. (2010) What Color is Your Parachute? http://www.amazon.ca/Color-Parachute-Retirement-Second-Edition/dp/158008205X

Pavey, S. "Personal Goal Setting". http://www.mindtools.com/page6.html

Sicinski, A. "Becoming a Big Thinker". http://blog.iqmatrix.com/habit-of-thinking-big

Smith, S. "A Guide to Evaluate Your Priorities & Set Goals". http://www.forbes.com/sites/samanthasmith/2013/12/30/a-guide-to-evaluate-your-priorities-set-goals/

Wax, D. "Back to Basics: Setting Priorities". http://www.lifehack.org/articles/productivity/back-to-basics-setting-priorities.html

Zulauf, C. (2001) The Big Picture: A Systems Thinking Story for Managers, Leaders, and Other Visionaries. http://www.amazon.com/The-Big-Picture-Thinking-Visionaries/dp/0967796555

Chapter Three:
Use Resources Wisely

Days are expensive. When you spend a day you have one less day to spend. So make sure you spend each one wisely.

~Jim Rohn

What Are Your Personal Resources?

Resources are innate and external things we have at our disposal to help us be successful in life. The first thing people think of when they hear the term resources is money. The second is often "natural resources".

Our resources might be organized in the following categories:

- Financial: Access to funds, money
- Natural: those things which occur in nature and are available to people
- Time: the physical space available to complete tasks
- Emotional: Resilience, stamina, ability to cope with life's problems

- Intellectual: Academic skills, learning, ability to read, write, communicate and compute
- Spiritual: Faith, religion, belief in a higher power, connection with things of a spiritual nature
- Physical: Health, fitness wellness
- Support Systems: Friends, family, formal and informal groups, facilities, organizations
- Mentors, Role Models: People who guide and influence
- Experience, Knowledge: Knowing the cultural rules of your society, manners, mores
- Social Skills: Ability to interact, relate to others

In Matthew 25:14-30 Jesus tells the Parable of the Talents. He uses this parable to caution people to make wise use of their personal resources.

> *For it will be like a man going on a journey, who called his servants and entrusted to them his*

property. [15] To one he gave five talents, to another two, to another one, to each according to his ability. Then he went away.[16] He who had received the five talents went at once and traded with them, and he made five talents more.[17]So also he who had the two talents made two talents more. [18] But he who had received the one talent went and dug in the ground and hid his master's money. [19] Now after a long time the master of those servants came and settled accounts with them. [20] And he who had received the five talents came forward, bringing five talents more, saying, 'Master, you delivered to me five talents; here I have made five talents more.[21] His master said to him, 'Well done, good and faithful servant. You have been faithful over a little; I will set you over much. Enter into the joy of your master.'[22]And he also who had the two talents came forward, saying, 'Master, you delivered to me two talents; here I have made two talents more.'[23] His master said to him, 'Well done, good and faithful servant. You have been faithful over a little; I will set you over much. Enter into the joy of your master. [24] He also who had received the one talent came forward, saying, 'Master, I knew you to be a hard man, reaping where you did not sow, and gathering where you scattered no seed, [25] so I was afraid, and I went and hid your talent in the ground. Here you have what is yours.[26] But his master answered him, 'You wicked and slothful servant! You knew that I reap where I have not sown and gather where I scattered no seed? [27] Then you ought to have invested my money with the bankers, and at my coming I should have received what was my own with interest. [28]So take the talent from him and give it to him who has the ten talents. [29] For to everyone who has will more be given, and he will have an abundance. But from the one who has not, even what he has will be taken away. [30] And cast the worthless servant into the outer darkness. In that place there will be weeping and gnashing of teeth.

While we are all blessed with talents of some sort, it is not a given that we all put those resources to good use. Some of us are too scared, lazy, or apathetic to use our God-given talents. In the Parable of the Talents, Jesus emphasizes the importance of the wise use of our resources. Otherwise, a talent is useless.

We all want to achieve great things in life. We want the perfect job, the perfect home, the ideal partner and dazzlingly brilliant children. However, most of us aren't getting the success we want in life. We want more money, more recognition, more romance and more joy in our lives. In truth, most of us aren't using our resources to achieve the success we desire.

Resources include: talents, strengths, skills, and even our time. Our resources, if utilized, can help us lead a happy, fulfilled, successful life. Whenever you are tempted to start worrying, think of something else positive and breathe a prayer of thanks. Start counting your blessings, then come back to the unpleasant situation and thank God, telling Him, that because he allowed it, he will also make a way of escape.

Two days ago, I came out of the bookshop and as I sat in my car, it dawned on me how horrible my morning had been. As I was tempted to start my day with unhappiness, I quickly realized the trick of the enemy. In this circumstance, he had come to steal my joy for the day. Ephesians 6:11 warns us to *Put on the full armor of God, so that you can take your stand against the devil's schemes {Tricks}* Parenthesis supplied.

Many a time, we look for big tricks of the devil, forgetting that the devil specializes in little things. Think about it. That is what actually makes it a trick because it is something we will normally overlook. The devil tries to trick us also into not making good use of our resources. Time is so valuable and is one of the most important resources.

Our talents can be as varied as an ability to play a sport, to cook a meal, to do a craft or hobby. Some of us have a talent of helping others, of encouraging or empowering others. Some of us use our personal time to help others. For some, the wise use of resources involves using our financial gifts to help those less fortunate. When you give a gift, you are actually crediting into your account of blessings. *Not that I seek the gift, but I seek the fruit that increases to your credit. Philippians 4:17*

Instead of making the most of our resources, we blame bad luck, poor timing, we finger point, blaming things that just "happen" to us, making life more complicated.

Greatness, success, the potential for the life we want exists in all of us. What we need to do is believe in ourselves, our abilities, our skills, our strengths, our resources. It is simply

up to us to pull it out of ourselves. While believing in ourselves, we must rely on God trusting that *I can do all things through Christ who strengthens me (Philippians 4:13).*

Despite the circumstances, the economic climate, and other impediments, we need to have faith that we are more powerful than we think. Look at the ant who moved the rubber tree plant. It was thousands his size but he had

THE DEVIL TRICKS US INTO NOT MAKING GOOD USE OF OUR RESOURCES. TIME IS ONE OF THE MOST IMPORTANT RESOURCES.

unfailing conviction in his abilities, his inner resources.

The little engine that could draw on his inner strength to chug to the top of what seemed an impossibly steep hill for such a small engine. David slew the mighty Goliath with just a slingshot and a stone. How did he do this? He had the talent of excellent marksmanship and the inner resources of a lion. He had faith in his God and his own abilities. When God was about to use Moses to deliver the children of Israel, He asked Moses "…what is that in your hand?" Exodus 4:2

Moses' answer to God's question was 'a shepherd's staff''. The shepherd's staff was Moses resource and God enabled him to use it to swallow Pharaoh's snakes, to part the red sea, and to do many other miracles. My question to you today is "what do you have in your hands?" meaning what are the strengths and abilities that God has given to you? These are your foundational resources. How are you using them?

Just as in the parable of talents, many bury their talents, skills, abilities, or knowledge. Successful and happy living is about using resources wisely. Using resources wisely means making intelligent choices. When we use our resources wisely, we get the most from whatever resources we have at our disposal: money, talent, skill, and emotional and physical properties.

Using your resources wisely may mean shopping around to make your financial resources go as far as you can make them go. Wise use of resources means getting a mortgage with the lowest interest or paying the least commission or having user fees waived. Using resources wisely involves maintaining a good credit score if you intend to take a loan for a business. When you fail to maintain a good credit score and becomes denied by lenders, do not think it is bad luck, take responsibility for what you did not do right.

If you want to achieve a 'don't worry be happy' state, you need to develop the following good habits:

1.Take Responsibility

Rather than blaming bad luck, poor help, the weather or anything else for our situation, we need to accept responsibility. This holds true of our successes too. We need to accept that it wasn't just a fluke of fortune or being in the right place at the right time that allowed us to succeed. Did the tortoise claim it was just luck that he defeated the speedy hare? No! He made wise use of his inner and outer resources and won the race!

Successful people take full responsibility for their good ideas, their clever thoughts, the images they visualize, and the actions they take. They neither blame nor deflect, accepting the responsibility for failures and successes.

Moreover, successful people see their failures as opportunities to learn, to revise, to fix, to change, to improve. They are not ashamed to admit their mistakes and learn from it. They do not also share their mistakes with everybody, only with like-minded people who will understand where they are coming from.

Successful people are not afraid to take risks to achieve the life they want to live. Let me pause to say here that it is necessary to take calculated risks, not just impulsive risks. An example is using your house rent to start a business and risk being thrown out of where you sleep. Why not risk your savings and not the things that determines your major needs of life.

a. Know What You Want in Life

Yogi Berra once quipped: "If you don't know where you're going, you'll wind up some place else."
Alice in Wonderland asked the Dormouse for directions. On hearing she didn't know where she wanted to go, he replied, "Then it doesn't matter which way you go."

God put us all in this world for a purpose. Unfortunately, many of us never take the time to ponder on our purpose. We are dissatisfied by our lives because we don't know what we want. If you don't know what you're supposed to be doing, look around you. Take stock. Look to others for help and guidance. Turn to your inner voice. Know yourself.
What are your personality traits? What are your likes and dislikes? What do you want out of life? What do you hope to accomplish?

Back in childhood, I dreamed of being a nurse, but I also admired business people. I knew as a child that business people made more than those on salary. I admired my mother running her small business of baking snacks like egg rolls, buns, meat or fish pies, etc. I watched as salesmen came to stock and leave our house every weekday morning, and how they came back in the evening to account money to my mother. Sometimes, she stocked our own containers and I went to sell the snacks accompanied by my sister Da Chinyeaka. As much as my parents taught I was helping to boost the family economy, a lot was going on in my mind. "What if this is done in a very large scale?" "That means a lot of money". Business was definitely something I was going to try out in the future.

When my father retired as a school teacher after 35 years of service, my parents decided to start their own private elementary school. With the help of my uncle, Dr Uzuegbu who provided the main chunk of the funding, this was made possible. I was actively involved in every step of starting the school.

I saw my father's faith that it was going to work as we went to Ihieorji council hall day after day to enroll prospective students into Wills Solid Foundation School. My father was a bit disappointed on the first day of school when we only had about 3 students. As I expressed my concern as to where all the students that had enrolled were, my father explained to me that people usually identify with success. The parents of the students were waiting to see that the school was successful before bringing in their kids. And that was exactly what happened.

Few weeks into resumption, the school was packed with students. Pre-school (Kindergarten) and Primary (Elementary) schools. I was in charge of the preschool section. My father placed me on a salary. At this time, I had just finished high school and was waiting to be admitted into the school of nursing. So, my waiting time was put into good use as I learned more the principles of business.

b. Put Your Goals on Paper

Write down your goals. This helps you refine them and provides a greater commitment to those goals.

Most of us are dissatisfied with our lives because we have no clear idea of what we want. We haven't made a decision.

We have failed to define our goals. We haven't identified what a successful life looks like.
Consequently, as Yogi put it, we end up some place else. We are vaguely disappointed. We know it wasn't where we wanted to be but we can't identify where we want to go. Like Alice in wonderland, we often have no idea where that desired spot is.

When I wanted to get married, I had certain traits I would like in a husband. I did not have any specific criterion as to whether the person should be fair in complexion or dark. My traits were: God fearing, handsome (not just in my eyes), someone who loves education, someone who believes the home should be a place where every member of the family has inner peace, someone who loves entrepreneurship, and someone who would not dream laying his hand on his wife no matter what the wife does. These traits, I can still remember. Having them in mind, I carefully scanned every spouse that came my way prayerfully, until God answered my prayer in May 2004.
I wrote a poem about my love and courtship relationship. You can easily find it on the internet. It is titled: The Seventh Man. Here it goes:

The Seventh Man (Part 1)

He was tall, he was black

He was deceitful, he was dishonest

He was the first

He was tall, he was black

He was adoring, he was amorous

He was the second

He was tall, he was black

He was a pastor, he was a parson

He was the third

He was tall, he was brown

He was a student, he was a speaker

He was the fourth

The Seventh Man (Part 2)

He was short, he was brown

He was so handsome, he was so homely

He was the sixth

He was tall, he was brown

He was so humble, he was so handsome

He was the seventh

He grapsed my hand

And did demand

From me my band

Of Honey gland

It was a grand

And hard demand

For me to hand

To him the gland

The Seventh Man (Part 3)

As he grew fonder

I had to ponder

And look to yonder

And also wonder

"Would there be an eight?"

"Do I have to wait?"

'Maybe just at seven
My young heart would leaven
My sweet womb would leaven'

I had to answer
The great Advancer

"Yes, take my honey gland
And be my sweet husband"

Someofjanespoetry.blogspot.com

c. Believe

Believe in yourself. Believe in your priorities. Believe in your ability to achieve them. Know what you bring to the task and what you want to achieve. As the saying goes, "If you believe it, you can achieve it!"
Remember you are not alone in your journey. Matthew 9:26 says: *Jesus looked at them and said, "With man this is impossible, but with God all things are possible."*

d. See Yourself Succeeding

In his book, *7 Steps for Creating the Life You Want* inspirational writer Jack Canfield suggests we see ourselves as "Inverse Paranoids". He further challenges: "Imagine how much easier it would be to succeed in life if you were constantly expecting the world to support you and bring you opportunity. Successful people do just that." They support other people and give other people opportunity.

e. Become a Goal Setter

Based on past experiences the brain tells us what is likely to happen. If you got a home run both times at bat, your brain tells you this is possible again. If you aced your mid-terms, the brain tells you that you will do fine on the finals.

Your mind has the power to psych you up for success. Unfortunately, it can also psych you out and you will be convinced you're never going to hit that high note or leap that hurdle. You have to believe it is possible or it is an unattainable goal. One thing that works for me in goal setting is that I always say it out to someone who understand everything I do and that is my husband. It is funny that sometimes when I set a goal, I may become lazy and he will be the one that asks me how it is going.

Some goals at first seem practically impossible. This is where optimism comes in. See yourself achieving those goals. Like the ant, visualize yourself moving that rubber tree plant. There is no end to the power of positive thinking. The mind is such a powerful instrument. It can deliver literally everything you want. Stories about miraculous feats accomplished because people believed that what they wanted—a medical degree, an Olympic gold medal, a cure for their cancer—was possible.

This power of the mind is faith in self, faith in a higher power (Jehovah) and unwavering belief in those resources you possess.

The reality is that those people who accomplished great things had a goal. You don't need a basket of goals. Often just one is enough to get you started. Out of goal setting comes a plan. Out of that plan to accomplish that goal comes action.

This is where setting priorities comes in. Having no goal is setting yourself up for defeat. You don't know where you're going. But having too many goals is overwhelming. Putting things in priority helps you make an immediate change in a single area. Ask yourself:

- ✓ What am I unhappy about in my life?
- ✓ How do I want it to change?

- ✓ What is my goal?
- ✓ What actions can I take to ensure that goal is achieved?
- ✓ What resources do I have to help me make this change?

f. Learn to Manage Time

In my book *How to Become a Better Wife*, I devoted one whole chapter to time management.
Time, like talent is a precious, finite resource. There is only so much of it available to each of us.
Why do some people seem to accomplish what they want to achieve while others never seem to have enough of this resource?

We all have the same amount of time. It's how we use this resource that makes the difference. In his book *Will It Make The Boat Go Faster?*, Olympic gold medalist Ben Hunt-Davis discusses how decisions that helped his team win gold at the Olympics were the result of asking themselves the crucial question: Will it make the boat go faster?

Time management will not put more hours in your day. However, it will help you accomplish more in the hours available to you.

The fact that there is a plethora of books on time management strategies is proof of the fact that people do not feel that they manage this resource wisely. A few particularly useful time management resources have been listed in the Useful Resources section at the end of this chapter.

Change is not easy. It's scary. It's risky. It often requires resources like time and money. Unless you believe this change is necessary, desirable, and achievable, there is no sense in trying.

Useful Resources

Allen, D. and Fallows, J. (2011) Getting Things Done: The Art of Stress-Free Productivity. http://www.amazon.com/Getting-Things-Done-Stress-Free-Productivity/dp/0143126563/ref=sr_1_1?s=books&ie=UTF8&qid=1435003838&sr=1-1

Brown Taylor, B. (2015) *Learning to Walk in the Dark.* http://www.amazon.com/Learning-Walk-Barbara-Brown-Taylor/dp/0062024345/ref=pd_bxgy_14_text_y

Canfield, J. (2007) *Key to Living: The Law of Attraction: A Simple Guide to Creating the Life of Your Dreams.* http://www.amazon.ca/Jack-Canfields-Key-Living-Attraction/dp/0757306586

Canfield, Jack. http://jackcanfield.com/7-steps-for-creating-the-life-you-want/11

Carroll, J. (2012) Time Management in Easy Steps. https://www.chapters.indigo.ca/en-ca/books/product/9781840785593-item.html?mkwid=sP8ld10FR_dc&pcrid=44154474422&pkw=&pmt=&s_campaign=goo-Shopping_Books&gclid=CjwKEAjw5J6sBRDp3ty_17KZyWsSJABgp-OaVxR9q-lrI0Kn4MpojBbqidutMLWqp6nqTwAjsWdjWBoCteXw_wcB

Dollar, C. (2009) *8 Steps to Create the Life You Want: The Anatomy of a Successful Life.* http://www.amazon.com/Steps-Create-Life-You-Want/dp/0446699640

Entrepreneur.com. "How to Manage Time with 10 Tips that Work". http://www.entrepreneur.com/article/219553

"How to Use Inner Resources to Make a Successful Life Change". http://podbay.fm/show/608009659/e/1364967606

Hunt-Davis, B. (2011) *Will It Make The Boat Go Faster?* *http://www.amazon.ca/Will-Make-Boat-Faster-Olympic-Winning/dp/1848769660*

Inner Drive.com. "Using Your Scarcest Resource Wisely". http://www.innerdrive.co.uk/Release_Your_Inner_Drive/using-scarcest-resource-wisely/

McLaren, B. (2015) *We Make the Road by Walking.* http://www.amazon.com/gp/product/1455514012/ref=amb_link_433429522_1?pf_rd_m=ATVPDKIKX0DER&pf_rd_s=hero-quick-promo-books-atf&pf_rd_r=0RZKQFVPREXZNFF57317&pf_rd_t=201&pf_rd_p=2102132142&pf_rd_i=0446699640

Mourdoukoutas, P. "The Six Rules of Personal Success". http://www.forbes.com/sites/panosmourdoukoutas/2012/02/11/the-six-rules-of-personal-success/

NC State University. "Identifying Personal Resources" in *Don't Go It Alone.* http://www.ces.ncsu.edu/depts/fcs/temp/Wellness/CurrModules/DontGoItAlone.pdf

Williams, K. and Reid, M. (2011). *Time Management.* https://www.chapters.indigo.ca/en-ca/books/product/9780230299603-item.html?mkwid=sAFdkUkBy_dc&pcrid=44154474422&pkw=&pmt=&s_campaign=goo-Shopping_Books&gclid=CjwKEAjw5J6sBRDp3ty_17KZyWsSJABgp-OaJUvudAqj0E-wedKA7fczGJDpi7AdDWTKa7XDUbPV0xoCoPHw_wcB

Chapter Four:
Learn to Focus

A habit is a cable; we weave a thread
each day and at last we cannot break it.

~Horace Mann

"How often have you told a child or a
spouse,
"Focus!"?

What Does it Mean to Focus?

When we focus, we pay attention to something. This might be an object. Hypnotists have their subjects focus on something shiny or moving. They do this to block out other stimuli so their subject's attention is solely on their voice.

When people meditate they often play soft music or chant. This is to blot out the world's distractions and focus on their inner self.

Our world is so full of distracting noises, and sights and thoughts that it is increasingly difficult to focus on one task, one person, one idea or one thought. We are so accustomed to multi-tasking that people of all ages have trouble with one single focus.

Why is Focusing Important to a Successful Life?

Staying focused means sticking with your priorities and goals; focusing on the message, not on the background noise; and executing. Take the right steps to reach your goals. That's all that matters in the end.

A HABIT IS THE REPETITION OF A BEHAVIOR. IF YOU PRACTICE THE PRINCIPLES OF SUCCESSFUL LIVING OVER AND OVER, UNCONSCIOUSLY, IT BECOMES A HABIT, YOU DO NOT EVEN HAVE TO THINK ABOUT IT .

It takes patience, persistence, and discipline to stay focused. Patience to overcome the hurdles that stand between you and your goal; persistence to overcome the failures, setbacks, and temptations that may take you off course; and discipline to play the game right, to comply with all the rules: know what you are doing, be punctual, and work out all the details. Successful people have successful habits. If you plan to be successful, you will be successful.

Life doesn't just happen to us. It is a series of choices. How we decide one day affects the choices we have to make the next day. If we make good choices, the decisions we have to make the next day are far different from the ones we have to make the following day. Making bad choices points us down the wrong road and makes it harder and harder to recover.

What Strategies Improve Focus?

In their book, *The Power of Focus*, authors Jack Canfield, Mark Victor Hansen, and Les Hewitt recommend that we concentrate on our strengths, set goals, and focus on these instead of dwelling on what we don't have and are not able to do.

The following are a few practical focusing strategies.

Strategy # 1: Establish Routines

Establishing routines frees you from making small but distracting decisions about:

- What time should I go to bed?
- What time should I get up?
- Will I shower in the morning or at night or both?
- What will I wear?

- Will I have breakfast?
- What will I eat?
- Do I need to pack a lunch?
- What route will I take to work?
- Did I bring home my brief case?

Sticking to daily routines frees your mind to focus on important things. You cannot have high levels of focus without routines to make your day productive. Your sleeping, eating, hygiene and dressing habits should be routine. This leaves more energy—and focus—for the day's challenges. I am not talking about being too stuck to routine that it starts dictating everything you do. For example, you have established to brush your teeth before you sleep and then in the middle of the night, you remember you did not do it tonight, so you jump out of bed to go and brush your teeth. If your system is like mine, it may take you a while to sleep back. Also being to stuck to routine may mean that you have developed an obsessive compulsive personality and may need a little mental help (sorry to be blunt).

When I started working nights shifts as a nurse (7pm to 7am), I quickly figured out that if I do not take my nap break around 11pm, the whole of the night would be useless.

As I made it a routine to take my nap break at 11pm, 1030pm or 1130pm, whichever time was available, I saw my nights going smoother because my brain would be awake the rest of the night.

Strategy # 2: Write it Down

Often we have difficulty focusing because too many things or people are competing for our attention. A good strategy is to jot down a phrase or keyword to remind yourself what you want to do or what you promised someone. Getting that out of the way also allows you to attend to other things. “Jotting” things down could be pencil and paper, planner, tablet or smart phone.

Strategy #3: Use a Mind Map

Some call this glorified doodling. Others find it very effective. A study in *Science* magazine shows that the human brain can handle two complicated tasks at the same time. Throw in a third one and your the brain is on overload. I don’t completely agree to that. I would say that you should only allow enough tasks as you can handle at a time. I can handle up to 5 tasks at a time, not be stressed about it and finish each one very successfully. So, it will depend on your brain, skills and comfortability capacity. Just know your limit.

If your brain has to handle too many things at the same time, you lose focus. That's when efficiency suffers. You lose track of one of the original tasks. There are oversights and errors—all because you are juggling too many balls at once. Jotting things quickly via pictures, symbols, shorthand…helps keep track of important information so nothing gets dropped.

Game coaches and players do this with a playbook. You might call this your "road map for the day". May I advice that you do not overdo this as the brain functions less when it is not challenged enough. What I mean here is that you try to remember somethings yourself without the paper.

Strategy #4: Shape Your Environment for Success

So often we simply put up with things that interfere with our focus—people who interrupt, ringing phones, beeping machines, sunlight streaming in across the desk, the hum of the air exchanger, buzzing flies, kids fighting… If we stopped to deal with these things the first time they were a distraction we'd have eliminated or at least dampened these sights, sounds and even smells that distract us from our job. But instead we soldier on even though we know these things and people are making us less effective!

For individuals with young kids like me, you should learn to do things that do not need kids' distraction when kids are not around. You can decide to do these tasks when kids are at school, or when they are sleeping. Training your kids not to distract you when you are serious with your work has not worked for me with the type of lovely children I have. On the other hand, I do not want to be the kind of mother that is always busy when my kids are around, so I always remember to give them ample attention while we are at home because family comes first before work.

Sometimes, sterile air or empty sound is a distraction. Perhaps a light aromatherapy or soft background music—or even the sound of a co-worker in the next office cubicle-can be soothing. Some people think working at home was distracting and unsettling because it was TOO quiet or because the sound of the washing machine was unfamiliar and thus distracting. It depends on the kind of work you are doing. Many people make thousands from home

You owe it to yourself and your success to decide what in your environment distracts you from your work and how to eliminate it. I have also trained my mind focus. It has helped me so much especially to sleep very soundly amidst a lot of noise around me.

It helped me during my night shifts and it also helps me almost every night because my husband always wants to watch a movie before he sleeps, and funny enough he likes to hold me lying down beside him, with him holding me in his arms and my head tilted to his breast like a baby, while he watches. Instead of complaining when I really need to sleep, I will put my head in his arms, tune my mind to sleep and sleep very comfortably.

Strategy #5: Put Things in Priority

A lot of what we do during the day is necessary but mind-numbingly boring. It's easy to put those tasks off and then knowing they are yet to be done distract you from the more pressing tasks.

Use that mind map to place the tasks—yes even the mind numbing ones—in priority so you have a productive day. Actually schedule your time to get those boring but essential jobs done.

Strategy # 6: Give Yourself Permission for a Quick Break

Do not try to complete a task as if your life depends on it. My mother always told me in my childhood, you are not tied to a rope to finish that now.

If those boring but essential tasks are messing with your productivity, give yourself permission to take short breaks. This might be a walk to the water cooler or rest room, a big stretch, a quick sip of cold water from your fridge. The pause will do wonders to get the blood flowing and allow you to dive back in.

When you finish a task, reward yourself with a five-minute break. But remember this is a quick break—not an excuse to procrastinate.

Strategy #7: Use Technology to Promote Punctuality

Nothing messes with your focus faster than worrying about being late. People have forgotten materials, names, entire presentations because being late—or sweating being late—caused them to lose focus. This is where technology can help. Use your GPS to calculate where you are going, how to get there and how long it will take. Program your phone to alert you when it's time to go. Set your alarm to make sure you don't sleep in. Use your tablet, smart phone or PDA to remind you what you need to take, find number, names of contacts, etc When I have an important appointment to keep early in the morning. I do not gamble with sleep, I use my alarm on my phone and I respect it.

Strategy #8: Build Rewards into Your Life

All work and no play make anyone dull, dreary, and cantankerous. Remember to build in social occasions—dinner, a movie, time with friends, a hobby, a trip, so you have something to look forward to. The anticipation builds focus and helps motivate you to complete a task. Do not be stingy when it comes to spending money on yourself.

The Bible says to love our neighbor as ourselves. Many a time, people do not notice that the statement contains two commandments: (a) Love yourself and (b) love your neighbor. Think about it: How can you love someone else when you do not actually love yourself? Jesus wants you to love yourself first, that is why He said to love our neighbors as we have loved ourselves because we should have done that first. Reward yourself with good food, good clothes, things you love and be happy. Do not be a shopaholic. I am not one and that is not what I am preaching here.

Always putting people first and always, and always neglecting yourself creates a life of worry and unhappiness. One of my relatives made sure all his kids went to the best schools.

He should have been in school while the kids also went to school at their own level. But in his selfless personality, he dropped out so his kids could finish and he never went back. Now, his kids are very successful and happy, but he is very unhappy because he could not achieve his life goals. That may be an extreme example, but I really devoted this part of this book to make sure you understand that rewarding yourself is part the strategies of leading a successful and happy life.

Strategy #9: Take Stock

Think about the times you can focus. What do those times have in common? Now think of the times you are unable to stay focused. What similarities do these occasions have? Make a list of your focusing strengths. Next, list things you have trouble doing to stay focused. Pick one weak area and decide how you can move it to a strength. When you have mastered that one, move on to another weak area and make it a strength.

I prefer working early in the morning when everyone is still sleeping to working late into the night. My husband is completely the opposite. He prefers to go to bed very late because he is working on his computer, while I prefer to go to bed very early and wake up in the night to work.

Take stock of what works for you and use it as your resource.

Strategy #10: Learn to Delegate

Part of what causes loss of focus is having too many things to think about. The important things get lost in the confusion. Worry and feeling overwhelmed doesn't make you effective. That is why this book is titled *Don't Worry Be Happy* because your state of mind has a lot to do with your achievement level.

Decide which tasks you personally need to do, which ones a colleague or family member can do, and which ones you will pay someone else to do.

Use your strengths. Know when someone else does something better—or just as well. It is a sign of good judgment—not weakness—to ask for help! As my businesses started growing, I came to realize the importance of delegation. I discovered that many tasks I usually wanted to do myself could as well be done by someone else when given instructions on what to do. That was when I learned the saying that one cannot become a millionaire by working alone.

People are looking for jobs and would efficiently do what you want them to do, not just for self-fulfillment, but also to keep their jobs.

In this age of the internet, instead of overwhelming yourself with tasks that could be done electronically, why not find a virtual assistant on the internet and give them such tasks to do, then pay them and keep your sanity? Simply search for virtual assistants online.

Strategy # 11: A Cluttered Desk is the Sign of a Cluttered Mind

If you want to maintain focus your workspace cannot look like your desk just exploded. Whether you're at work in an office, a hotel room, your car, or telecommuting your workspace has to be organized so you can find everything immediately. If your workspace is clean, you focus on what is important and get your work done with much more concentration. Get rid of distractions. File or discard what isn't immediately important. Dump irrelevant do dads. Your desk should include only what you need to do your job.

Strategy #12: Manage Your Time

I have dwelt on this earlier in the book. We all have the same number of hours in a day. Those who think they haven't enough time are often unaware of how they use—or misuse—their time. Managing your time fits perfectly with creating a to-do list or a mind map.

Beside each item on the list or map, estimate how long you need to accomplish it. Try to complete each task within that time frame. This will allow you to focus on each task with a sense of purpose.

Strategy #13: Know Why You are Doing what You are Doing

If we have a sense of purpose for what we are doing it helps us focus on the task. Sometimes you need to ask a colleague or superior why you are doing what you have been asked to do. Knowing how the task fits into the giant plan of things helps you focus on completing that task. Find your purpose. Having a purpose to finish motivates and keeps you focused. We lose focus if we can't see the point of completing a task. That purpose can be the key that unlocks the door to your focus.

Strategy #14: Establish Goals

Ask yourself: *Why is this task worth completing?* Set goals so you have a focus on the future and a "prize" at the end. Goals may be individual or group. Your goals may be home or work-related. They may be lofty—like making the world a better place—or basic—like feeding and sheltering your family.

Without goals we are merely going through the motions without focus on the future.

Strategy #15: Pace Yourself

While setting goals helps you focus, having too many goals ensures you will be scattered and unfocused. Pick one, two or three big goals that you plan to accomplish. If you set too many you will overwhelm yourself and accomplish little. At the beginning of this year, my husband and I set about 8 big goals and we wrote them down, prayed on them and started acting on them. It is about 6 weeks to the end of the year, and by God's grace, we only have one big goal left. Big goals are different from small goals that you set as you go along. Take stock of what you have accomplished and what you still need to do.

Strategy #16: Build Your Focus Muscle

Just like any other skill we do, get better at focusing with practice. Every one of us can become more focused and less easily distracted with commitment and motivation. Start with short tasks like thirty minutes. When you are able to focus for shorter periods, work up to longer periods and more concentrated tasks.

Strategy #17: Read

Reading is one of those activities which demands focus—if you plan to remember what you've read. Reading challenges you to stay focused on just that task. Doing reading tasks can improve your focus. Start with a specific number of pages or a specific number of minutes to read each day. Choose something you are interested in: the newspaper, a magazine, a novel, a graphic novel or a non-fiction book. What you read isn't the important thing. Focusing on what you are reading and tuning out the distractions is the important part. I read a lot, not just because I write books, but because I constantly invest in self-development. Reading self-development books and writing my books are my hobbies.

Strategy #18: Make Changes to what You Eat

This may seem totally unrelated to staying focused. How can what you eat or drink change your ability to focus? Well it can. Too much caffeine in drinks or food can cause difficulty staying focused—or even sitting still to focus! Foods containing refined sugars have the same effect. Chocolate also causes some people to get jittery or hyperactive.

Not having enough water is also a cause of lack of focus. Avoid sports drinks, fruit smoothies and iced drinks. They are high in sugar and may also contain stimulants like caffeine. Drink at least 64 ounces (8 glasses) of water a day.

Instead of three large meals, try eating six smaller ones. That keeps your sugar levels even and helps you focus. Don't skip breakfast. It's important to help you keep focused. Unless you are fasting and praying, do not skip breakfast. Don't eat breakfast because you are hungry, as you won't be hungry enough to eat in the morning if your system is like mine. Eat breakfast because it is the healthy thing to do. Eat light breakfast and set your system to focus for the day.

Strategy #19: Consider Your Learning Style

How do you receive and process information best? Are you someone who sees things and remembers them? Do you learn best by hearing things? Are you a kinesthetic-tactile

learner who needs to physically write thing down or manipulate materials in order to comprehend and remember? Figure out how you learn best. Then organize your environment and the tasks before you so they accommodate the way you learn best. This will improve your focus.

Strategy #20: Learn to say, "No!"

Part of being focused involves knowing what you must do and what you want to do. When someone approaches you with a new task, don't agree to do it if it is not something you feel you must do or something you really want to do AND have the time to do. Pick and choose deliberately. Declutter your responsibilities. Don't let people guilt you into tasks you do not have time for. This will cause you to lose focus on what you must do.

Learn to say, "No!" firmly, decisively, and with a clear conscience. You will command more respect when you say 'No' to a task, than when you say 'Yes' and not deliver.

Strategy # 21: Use Mental Rehearsal

Visualize what you want to do or say. See yourself achieving the desired results. Get a clear mental image of you in action, achieving success. See yourself circumventing obstacles.

Watch a mental video of you adroitly leaping hurdles. Feel the success and fulfillment knowing you did a good job. Feel the elation and excitement and, yes, relief that the job is done. This mental rehearsal gets you focused and puts you in the right frame of mind to accomplish the task.

Strategy #22: Increase Your Will Power

Focus requires self-control. You have to learn to resist the lure of short-term pleasures in temptations in favour of long-range gains.

You can increase your willpower by using such techniques as: meditation, mindful breathing, visualization, and biofeedback. Regular meditation you can boost your willpower. These "mindful activities give you incentive for taking deliberate, focused action. Being mindful of what is going on in your body increases your willpower and helps you stay focused, undistracted by noise going on in your head or emotions bubbling up inside you.

Strategy #23: Finish What You Started

We live in a world of distractions. People are constantly multitasking—texting and driving and talking on the phone and drinking coffee. If you want to be focused you need to deal with one thing at a time. Don't start something new until you've finished what you are doing. This statement is ambiguous. I will explain what I mean.

I am a multi-tasker, but I always remember my unfinished tasks and go back to them. The point I am trying to make here is that you should not be jack of all trades and master of none. Only be jack of the trades you can be a master of. Always do your best to complete every single task you start. The best outcomes are the result of concerted, single-minded focus on the task at hand.

Strategy #24: Aim to Create an Automatic Response

Routines allow focus on other decisions. Making a lot of what you do in a day—getting up, getting dressed, going to work, checking email, creating a to do list—automatic means you are not expending a lot of mental or physical energy on activities you don't need to waste time on. Routines, delegating duties, doing things automatically, creating lists all help you maintain focus on what needs your undivided attention.

Useful Resources

Canfield, J., Hansen, M. J. and Hewitt, L. (2012). *The Power of Focus: Tenth Anniversary Edition: How to Hit Your Business, Personal, and Financial Targets with Absolute Confidence and Certainty.* *http://www.amazon.ca/Power-Focus-Tenth-Anniversary-Edition-ebook/dp/B0079K5NHO*

Entrepreneur.com. "How to Stay Focused: Train Your Brain". http://www.entrepreneur.com/article/225321

Goins, J. "How to Stay Focused while Writing". http://goinswriter.com/how-to-stay-focused-writing/

Goodwin, B. and Hubbell, E. The 12 Touchstones of Teaching: Staying Focused Every Day. http://www.ascd.org/Publications/Books/Overview/The-Twelve-Touchstones-of-Good-Teaching.aspx

Gray, J. (1988). *Staying Focused in a Hyper World Book 1: Natural Solutions for ADHD, Memory, and Brain Performance.* http://www.amazon.ca/Staying-Focused-Hyper-World-Performance-ebook/dp/B00MC3SP78

Guise, S. "How to Get Focused Anywhere in 5 Minutes". http://deepexistence.com/how-to-get-focused-anywhere-in-5-minutes/

Jaeger, A. (2000) Getting Focused Staying Focused. http://www.amazon.ca/Getting-Focused-Staying-Alan-Jaeger/dp/1881643239

Morris, R. "10 Tips: How to Stay Focused through the Coming Year" http://bigthink.com/experts-corner/10-tips-how-to-stay-focused-through-the-coming-year

Chapter Five:

Form Meaningful Relationships: Treasure Friendships

Cherish your human connections - your relationships with friends and family.
~Barbara Bush

Forming meaningful relationships is a basic human need. Friendships and other meaningful relationships help make a life successful and enriched. In order to do this, people need to be aware of several facts about meaningful relationships:

- People who have a better understanding of themselves form relationships easier. When meeting others they are less stressed, more relaxed and more confident. Strive for self-knowledge. You understand others to the degree you understand yourself.

- If a relationship is meaningful, the behavior of other people in that relationship should not determine how you feel about yourself and the others.

- Don't form opinions of people by what they say or do but rather because of what causes them to behave as they do.

- To have a fulfilling relationship, you need to stop living timidly, fearing what others will think of you. What you think of yourself is what's important.

- If a friendship requires you to be someone you are not, then it isn't a meaningful relationship. As Adrian Savage author of, *LifeHack* points out: "If you can't trust yourself, why should others trust you?"

- Real relationships are symbiotic. We cannot hurt others without hurting ourselves.

- Having a mature relationship means you do not have to defend yourself or your actions. Many a time when I do something, my husband already knows why I took that action. I don't do a lot of explaining, just as he does not do because we are in a healthy relationship. In healthy relationships, there are not a lot of defenses because your partner already knows your weaknesses. You may want to buy my book *How to Become a Better Wife* and also another book, I co-authored with my husband *How to Become a Better Husband.*

- In every relationship there will be ups and downs, highs and lows, happiness and disappointment. To shelter yourself from the lows of a relationship is to deny yourself the joy of the highs. "If they never make you cry, they'll never make you laugh."

- Every unpleasant experience with another person is an opportunity to learn about relationships. It's a chance to see people as they are, not as we like to think they are.

- We will not recognize and appreciate in others virtues we do not ourselves possess.

How to Form Meaningful Relationships

When it comes to forming meaningful relationships, several principles prevail:

1. **Our relationships with others are a reflection of the relationship we have with ourselves.**

If you believe in giving of yourself, you will believe others have your best interests at heart. If, on the other hand, you feel you should guard your feelings, you will be miserly in sharing your time, talents, and feelings with others. They in turn will not be warm and outgoing toward you.

2. **Focus on unconditional giving.**

Do you have friends with whom you felt an instant connection? Are there people you disliked immediately upon meeting? How do you decide?

3. **Relationships develop in three layers:**

- What you see on the outside.
- What happens in the conscious minds of you and the other person.
- What is happening in the subconscious minds of both people.

If our focus is on unconditional giving, we unconsciously reflect this in body language, tone of voice, and the diction in our dealings with others. We are approachable, inviting. Others gravitate toward us.

4. **Treat others as they want you to treat them.**

This goes beyond the Golden Rule: "Do unto others as you would have them do unto you." This assumes what's best for us will be what others want in a relationship. Instead, commit to discovering what others want, and strive in a meaningful relationship to give that to them.

5. **Meaningful relationships have give and take.**

Relationships are a two-way street. Both people have to be giving and taking. If one is predominantly the giver and the other the receiver, then it's not a relationship. Both parties in a relationship must be prepared to let the other give and take.

6. Meaningful relationships are about empathy.

We all have our own experiences. However, for a relationship to be meaningful, we need to be able to see things from the other's view. We need to be able to empathize. We need to understand how the other sees the world. Until

> RELATIONSHIP IS A TWO-WAY THING. EVERY PARTNER MUST BE GIVING AND TAKING, IF ONLY ONE PARTNER IS GIVING OR TAKING, THE RELATIONSHIP IS NOT HEALTHY.

you can empathize with others, you are not truly building a relationship.

Empathizing involves listening actively to the other person. As George P. H. points out in *Pick The Brain*, connecting with people means hearing them without interrupting and putting yourself in the other's position. "Walk a mile in his shoes."

7. **Meaningful relationships bring emotional safety.**

One of our jobs in a meaningful relationship is to ensure others feel safe. If it is a real relationship, we can bring others into a place where it is emotionally safe to open up, to share, to form real bonds.

8. **Accept all behavior unconditionally**

Behavior is driven by pain and pleasure. Humans always make the best available choice given two alternatives. Sometimes it is a tough decision between two great choices. Sometimes the hard decision is the less painful of two hard choices. Regardless of the outcome, you have to understand the motivation. This doesn't excuse hurtful behaviour. However, it does allow you to empathize with others. If they had a more pleasurable option, they would take it. Thus, you need to accept the behaviour as their available option. I have also grown to understand that people act based on their level of knowledge.

Before you become upset at someone's behaviour, have you asked yourself "How much about this situation does this individual know?" When I see the reaction of some people in certain situations, I try to imagine myself at that level of ignorance. Sometimes, I connect, sometimes, I don't, but I try to be as professional as I can. Also, sometimes people have a bad day and just need to vent. In a meaningful relationship, you're prepared to be a "punching bag" for that moment.

9. If you are to be happy in a relationship, you need first to be happy within.

Michelle Maros author of, *Peaceful Mind Peaceful Life*, states, "Your relationships outside will flounder if you don't have unconditional love and compassion for yourself." To be a good friend to others you must first love yourself. Being positive and upbeat enriches and solidifies relationships. Barbara Fredrickson, a psychologist at the University of North Carolina, encourages optimism and a happy outlook on life. In her article in *Psychology Today*, she talks about "social positivism". When you see a glass with water halfway, do you see it as half-full or half-empty?

Be proactive in cultivating relationships.

Don't wait for the other to make a move. If you feel there's a connection, professionally or personally, be proactive. As author Keith Ferrazzi says in *Never Eat Alone*, follow up within 48 hours. Strike while the iron is hot.

10. Take stock of what you already have.

Some relationships are long-term. Some just weren't intended to be long lasting. Geographically, or emotionally, or logistically you and that other person were "two ships that passed in the night". Please, I am not talking of 'one night stands'. Sometimes relationships which were probably better as short-term linger. One or both of you cling to the relationship because it is comfortable, familiar or safe. These are the relationships you need to let go. Letting go of relationships that are really serving no one provides the opportunity for new relationships to develop. Sometimes, it's a matter of rekindling old relationships that have lapsed and now once again mutually meaningful.

11. Find common interests.

If you have little in common, what is the basis for the relationship? Relationships develop because of shared experiences, shared interest, and/or shared goals.

12. Learn to trust.

All relationships require trust. If you cannot learn to trust, then the relationship is doomed. I cannot imagine myself living a life of stalking my husband, checking his cell phones, eaves dropping into his phone calls, checking his emails, etc. I am not bragging about the trust I have in him, I just give God the glory that I am in a relationship with someone I trust. My husband on the other hand trusts me so much, that sometimes, I am so afraid to betray his trust.
He trusts that every word I tell him is true so much that if he asks me a question that I know the answer will cause problem at that time, I will just tell him, "I will tell you at better time".

13. Know what you want and expect from a relationship.

No one likes to be disappointed. You will never get your needs fulfilled if you don't:

- Know what you need and expect from a relationship.

- Make it clear to others what your needs and wants are.

Honesty might be uncomfortable and scary but it is an absolute necessity in a relationship.

14. Understand what is being expected of you in a relationship.

This isn't always as simple as it may appear. As Steve Boyer points out, "People will always ask different questions. These are often not the ones they want you to answer." You need to be able to read between the lines and discover what is actually being asked of you.

Useful Resources

Boyer, S. "Unbox Love". http://www.unboxlove.com/

Ferrazzi, K. (2005) Never Eat Alone and Other Secrets to Success: One Relationship at a Time. http://www.amazon.com/dp/B000FCJZ4K/ref=rdr_kindle_ext_tmb

Fredrickson, B. (2009) POSITIVITY: GROUNDBREAKING RESEARCH REVEALS HOW TO EMBRACE THE HIDDEN STRENGTH OF POSITIVE EMOTIONS, OVERCOME NEGATIVITY, AND THRIVE. http://www.amazon.com/Positivity-Top-Notch-Research-Reveals-Upward-ebook/dp/B001NLKWUI

Howard, V. "Twenty Special Secrets," from *Mystic Path to Cosmic Power*.(1999). http://www.amazon.ca/The-Mystic-Path-Cosmic-Power/dp/0911203400

Maros, M. *Peaceful Mind Peaceful Life*. *http://peacefulmindpeacefullife.org/blog/*

P. H., George. "5 Ways to Stay Happy no Matter what Happens". http://www.pickthebrain.com/blog/author/george-p-h/

Rampton, J. 25 Tips for Having Meaningful Relationships". http://www.entrepreneur.com/article/241217

Thegivegive.com. "7 Principles of Meaningful Relationships". http://thegivegive.com/7-principles-of-meaningful-relationships/

Chapter 6:

Practice the Golden Rule: Do Unto Others as You'd Have Them Do Unto You

THOU SHALT LOVE THY NEIGHBOR AS THYSELF.

~Leviticus 19:18

Jesus taught us several lessons about living the Golden Rule. In the Sermon on the Mount, he said**:** "All things whatsoever ye would that men should do to you, do ye even so to them." The Mosaic Law echoes this commandment: "Whatever is hurtful to you, do not do to any other person."

In Matthew 7:12, it says, **"**If you then, being evil, know how to give good gifts to your children, how much more will your Father who is in heaven give what is good to those who ask Him! In everything, therefore, treat people the same way you want them to treat you, for this is the Law and the Prophets."

In Matthew 22:39 Jesus said, "This is the great and foremost commandment. The second is like it, 'YOU SHALL LOVE YOUR NEIGHBOR AS YOURSELF. On these two commandments depend the whole Law and the Prophets."

One of the key principles of getting along with people is the Golden Rule. The Golden Rule helps you relate to people. It is a guide to follow behaviour.

Many religions share this life philosophy. It provides a basic approach to interaction with others. The Bible says: "As you wish that others would do to you, do so to them" (Luke 6:31).

What does treating others as you wish to be treated have to do with your happiness?

You may be at this moment scratching your head and saying to yourself: *But what does this have to do with MY happiness?* It has a lot to do with the title of this book *Don't Worry Be Happy*

Treating others as you would want to be treated in their place will ultimately lead to your own happiness because you will have peace. You will not have to start doing one thing or another to cover the wrong you have done. You will not have to start telling a lie to cover another lie. You will not have to start working hard to re-establish lost trust.

I think one of the greatest gifts from God I cherish is Peace of Mind. Many a time, it comes by making others happy.

Living the Golden Rule is a long-standing standard of behaviour for many cultures. It involves showing respect for one another and treating others with dignity and respect.

The Golden Rule is not always easy to follow. This is particularly so when the going gets tough. Economic downturn, shortages of food or gas or money, disasters such as hurricanes, floods, blizzards and earthquakes bring out the "survival of the fittest" and "every man for himself" attitude. In times of trouble we become egocentric and selfish protecting what we have.

How do we practice The Golden Rule?

First take stock. Think about what the Golden Rule means for you. Others will gladly interpret it for you. That's not the way it should be. What does the Golden Rule mean for you? How can you best express it in your words and your actions? Be clear about how the Golden Rule guides your interactions. Once you know this, it is easier to practice the Golden Rule in your daily life. Then you are free to read and learn about the various interpretations of ways of enacting them and it must be workable for you. Think about:

- How do you want to treat others?
- What motivates the things you do and say to others?

- When have you known you should be kinder, more compassionate or more interested?
- What stops you from behaving toward others the way you know you should?
- When you fail to live by the Golden Rule, how do you get back on track?

1. **Be empathetic**.

Try to put yourself in the other person's shoes. Whether it's a family member, an employee, a colleague, your child's teacher or the neighbor across the street, try to imagine what it is like to be that person. What are they are going through? What stuff are they dealing with? How does it feel to be them? Why do they behave the way they do? The more you can empathize, the better you can practice the Golden Rule.

2. Be **compassionate**.

Once you can understand another person, and feel what they're going through, the next step is to have a desire to help them. Being compassionate involves searching for ways to help people, to ease their suffering, to be there for them and, if possible, to help them find solutions to their problems.

We all—at one time or another—go through bad times. Often when we do, we lash out at those around us. Knowing this and not taking those attacks personally is all part of showing compassion for someone who is hurting. It doesn't mean we have to become a doormat or whipping boy. It just means we KNOW why the person is lashing out and we make allowances because it is all part of being compassionate. For married people, when your spouse becomes touchy for no reason, instead of adding salt to pepper, why not stand back and try to see the reason behind this attitude?

Remember: This is in no way a reflection on your worth or even what the person actually thinks of you. They are hurting so they lash out. You should opt to take their reactions personally. You could cut them adrift as a friend or lash out at them. However, part of being compassionate is rising above what they say or do with the knowledge of why they are behaving that way. Both you and they will be happier if you can overlook their less-than-grateful response. Instead of being bitter or vengeful, seek to help the other person find a way to healing. Don't harbor grudges, or build up defenses. Use compassion to try to see the situation from the other's viewpoint.

Think about why a person has reacted poorly and stop before you react in kind. In Ephesians 4:32 Jesus said, "Be kind to one another, tenderhearted, forgiving one another, as God in Christ forgave you.

3. **Ask Yourself:** ***How would I want to be treated if I were that person?***

Go beyond "as you would have them do unto you." Instead, try to imagine how the other person would want to be treated. Ask yourself how you would want to be treated if you were in their situation.

In 1 John 4:20 Jesus said, *If anyone says, "I love God," and hates his brother, he is a liar; for he who does not love his brother whom he has seen cannot love God whom he has not seen. And this commandment we have from him: whoever loves God must also love his brother.*

President Kennedy showed his ability to see how others would want to be treated during the difficult days of de-segregation in the 1960s. He asked white Americans to imagine being looked down upon and treated badly based on color.

To imagine themselves in the situation of African Americans. Then he asked them to act accordingly towards the blacks.

4. Be friendly

Following the Golden Rule means treating others—known and strangers—in a friendly manner. This does not mean falling all over people trying to be their best friend. It means being friendly within socially appropriate bounds. For children it means being polite to adults but not being too trusting. For adults it means being civil and helpful and cheerful—not trying to make everyone your best friend.

Whether you are an adult dealing with children, peers, colleagues or seniors, being friendly means treating everyone you meet with respect, whether you know the people you're interacting with or not. In Romans 12:20 we are told to Love one another with brotherly affection. Outdo one another in showing honor.

Being friendly at any age is a question of good manners. Manners in any culture are helpful guidelines for acceptable ways to interact with others politely and kindly. Manners dictate—without our even having to give it a second thought—how we should treat others. We should have learned them within our family and social circle as we were growing up. By adulthood they should be automatic.

5. Be helpful.

As a society, we fail miserably at this part of The Golden Rule. We could learn valuable lessons from the Amish or Mennonite societies. Many people who go out of their way to be helpful. But, in general, as we have become less a rural and more an urban society, we have tended to keep more to yourself. We neither know about—or care about—the situation of those who live mere yards from us. The improvement of technological gadgets is not helping matters. People hear their cell phone ring, but do not bother answering the phone because they don't feel like talking, but immediately they hear a text message beep, they quickly rush to check their phones because they prefer to text than call; they prefer to deal with inanimate objects, than human beings.

The Golden Rule tells us not to ignore the problems of others. We shouldn't be blind to the woes and needs of others close to or far away from us.

Instead, we should seek ways help without being asked because we feel that it is the right thing to do.

In Matthew 25 35-40, we are told:

For I was hungry and you gave me something to eat, I was thirsty and you gave me something to drink, I was a stranger and you invited me in, I needed clothes and you clothed me, I was sick and you looked after me, I was in prison and you came to visit me.'

Then the righteous will answer him, 'Lord, when did we see you hungry and feed you, or thirsty and give you something to drink? When did we see you a stranger and invite you in, or needing clothes and clothe you? When did we see you sick or in prison and go to visit you?'

The King will reply, "Truly I tell you, whatever you did for one of the least of these brothers and sisters of mine, you did for me."

6. **Avoid road rage**.

With urbanization and long commutes to work, and increased traffic, road rage has become an unfortunate bi-product. Road rage is the epitome of unkindness and selfish juvenile behavior. It shows a complete lack of empathy, consideration and respect. Drivers appear to leave the Golden Rule behind them whenever they get behind the wheel of a vehicle. They refuse to yield, run yellow lights, cut one another off, honk and shout and make rude gestures. Courtesy on the road is a long lost art. If you want to judge the kind of person you are, check what comes out of your mouth or your reaction whenever you encounter a bad driver.

7. **Listen to others.**

We all want to talk. Few want to listen. When we do listen, we often don't heed what the other person is saying. With all the technology active listening—really hearing—seems to have become a lost art. There is something I have termed 'listening disability'. It is the inability to shut one's mouth and listen to the other speaker. You tend to finish the other person's statement thinking you already know what they have in mind. How many times have you tried finishing someone's statement and they told you that was not what they wanted to say? How did you feel?

Take the time to actually listen. Don't just wait your turn to talk. Use your ears to hear what the other person is going through. Read between the lines. Often there's a hidden message.

But you will never know if you don't pay attention to what is being said—and not said.

8. **Overcome prejudice**.

We all have our prejudices. I guess that is one of the sinful attributes of human beings. But, we need to be aware that these ARE prejudices and deal with them accordingly. We can't assume ALL black people or lawyers or tall people or blonds or fat people are the same. Try to see each person as a unique being. Instead of focusing on what makes them different from you, focus on how we are alike in spite of our different backgrounds, needs, skin color, language, race or religion.

9. **Don't be critical**.

It's easy to criticize others—colleagues, friends, neighbors, relatives and even celebrities. *Ask yourself: Would I like to be treated this way by others? How would it make me feel?*

Withhold your criticism, and only do it when it is unavoidable. Deal with others positively. Others think more highly of you and you think more highly of yourself if you don't pick apart the people and things around you.

10. **Don't control others**.

No one wants to be controlled. There was a research about how people react when they feel they are being controlled. In one hospital, they asked all the nurses to put their ID cards on their chest. Just because that announcement was made, many nurses started clipping their ID cards at the tip of their scrubs or on the hip pockets, even those who would naturally clip it on their chest pockets, just to revolt that they should be allowed to clip their ID cards wherever they chose. When the administration noticed what was happening, they did not mention it again. As time went on, the workers gradually started clipping it on their chest pockets, knowing they were no longer obligated to position their ID cards.
As silly as this reaction was, it simply demonstrates that people do not like control. When you get the urge to control, think how you would feel if others treated you this way. Reach consensus. Collaborate. Discuss. Reach an agreement instead of making it a standoff. Practice being flexible.

We like to control situations and others because we fear the unknown. Interacting with others successfully requires compassion, active listening, empathy and flexibility.

Be open-minded. Suspend judgment and find out about others' interests, abilities and talents. Don't push your preference and interests on them. By listening and withholding judgment you gain the respect of others—and often find out new things yourself.
When you approach others with curiosity and open mindedness, when you don't try to control, others are more willing to listen to your ideas.

11. **Be a child**.

Now this sounds weird, doesn't it. But I am not asking you to be immature. Children have a natural open mindedness and flexibility. They are color blind when it comes to prejudice. They are not critical of others. Remember what it was like to be a child.

12. Remind yourself.

Until it becomes second nature to us, we need reminders to live by the Golden Rule. Here are some effective ways to do this:

Set a golden rule reminder alarm on your phone to beep at a particular time of the day.

Email yourself a daily reminder.

Use Google Calendar or memotome.com to set up reminders of The Golden Rule, so you don't forget.

Have a wallpaper reminder on your computer.

Post a note on the fridge or bathroom mirror or your locker at work.

Put up a Golden Rule poster like this:

Photo courtesy of pixbay.com

Create a reading list based on the Golden Rule. A good source about inspirational Golden Rule stories is: http://www.values.com/your-inspirational-stories

Read to your kids about the Golden Rule. Good choices include:

Bernstein Bears and The Golden Rule

The Golden Rule by Ilene Cooper

Read about people who tried hard to live by the Golden Rule like:

- Jesus
- Mother Teresa
- Ghandi
- Dr. Martin Luther King Junior
- Buddha
- Joan of Arc
- Confucius
- Hammurabi
- Socrates
- Isocrates
- Epicurus
- Jean Jacques Rousseau
- Plato

13. **Rise above retaliation**.

It's human nature to strike back when someone strikes at us. The Golden Rule isn't about retaliation. It's about treating others as we'd want to be treated.

This does not mean we should let people run over us. We have a right to be treated with respect. We can assert that right without being aggressive or mean. Assert your rights. But do so while treating others fairly.

14. **Be the change**.

One of my favorite sayings comes from Gandhi who told us to be the change we want to see in the world. When people see this quote they always envision finding a cure for poverty or AIDS. Small changes and small interactions between people can make important changes too. If you think treating people with compassion is important, be a role model for doing just that. Let the change start with you. Even if the world doesn't change, at least you have made a start like the New Yorker who was bringing love back to the city.

One of Art Buchwald's friends lavished praise on strangers because he was certain it made the world a better place. To five construction workers he said: *"that's a magnificent job you men have done. it must have been difficult and dangerous work."* to a cab driver: *"thank you for the ride. you did a superb job of driving."*

When questioned about what he was doing the man simply said, "*i believe i have made that taxi driver's day. suppose he has 20 fares. he's going to be nice to those 20 fares because someone was nice to him. those fares in turn will be kinder to their employees or shopkeepers or waiters or even their own families. eventually the goodwill could spread to at least 1,000 people. now that isn't bad, is it?*"

He's right. It's the ripple effect. Like a pebble in a pond, his small act could send out large ripples.

15. **Notice how the way you treat others makes you feel**.

Be sensitive to how your actions affect others—especially when you treat them with kindness, compassion, respect, trust, or love. How does this make you feel better about yourself? Changes may come slowly. But, if you pay attention, you'll see them. It just gives you inner joy, peace and fulfillment.

16. **Realize the wider benefits of living the Golden Rule.**

Spread the attitude of living the Golden Rule. Plant seeds of kindness and respect and you will be rewarded for your kind acts. When you live by the Golden Rule, you set a standard and are a role model for others. Your action and words gives others motivation and conviction to live their life that way too.

The Golden Rule is contagious. The more people adhere to the Golden Rule the more others see the positive effects and want to emulate those acts. This prayer on the Golden Rule is attributed to Eusebius of Caesarea

> *May I gain no victory that harms me or my opponent.*
> *May I reconcile friends who are mad at each other.*
> *May I, insofar as I can, give all necessary help to my friends and to all who are in need.*
> *May I never fail a friend in trouble.*

Why Don't More People Practice the Golden Rule?

Applying the Golden Rule in your workplace sounds good on paper. However, in the cold, hard light of reality it is hard to sustain day after day in the face of negativity.

The Golden Rule is simple and flexible. After some time, it becomes—like good manners—second nature. The Golden

Rule is applicable to any situation—domestic or professional.

The Golden Rule provides an effective guide on how to be a friend. Friends are people who care about you, share in your joys and pain. If you want someone to be there for you, to laugh and cry with, then you need to do treat them this way. Friendship is a two-way street and that is the lesson The Golden Rule teaches us about interpersonal relations.

Why is this so difficult a concept to grasp? If everyone lived by the Golden Rule, there would be no wars, no conflict or hurts. People don't always know how to treat themselves. Consequently, they treat others poorly too. Learning the Golden Rule as an adult takes time. If children are raised in a family and community that treats one another according to the Golden Rule then it is already second nature to them.

When the person realizes what it takes to be a true friend, behaviors change. Strong friendships develop.

People dismiss the Golden Rule because they fail to realize the benefits to themselves of giving to others. They see generosity as a liability. They see no return on giving to others.

It was interesting to me to see how Apostle Paul asked the early Christians for help. He told them that he was not asking for their help, but he was asking them to give him because when they did, they would have a credit in their bank account in heaven. Phillipians 4:17. So, when you help someone, you are actually depositing into your account with God.

Used as a philosophy of life, The Golden Rule has many benefits to the giver and the receiver. Those who do not see the benefits need to be the recipients of the compassion, empathy, kindness and understanding of those who espouse the Golden Rule as their base for behavior. Only then can they be changed, one person at a time, to believe this is the way to achieve success in life.

Useful Resources

Babauta, L. "18 Practical Tips for Living the Golden Rule". http://zenhabits.net/18-practical-tips-for-living-the-golden-rule/

Birnbach, C. "The Golden Rule: Treating People as You'd Like to be Treated". http://friendship.about.com/od/Keeping-Friendships-Strong/g/The-Golden-Rule.htm

Buscaglia, L. (1985) *Living, Loving & Learning*. http://www.amazon.ca/Living-Loving-Learning-Leo-Buscaglia/dp/0449901815

Goulston, M. "Do You Practise the Golden Rule?" in *Psychology Today* *https://www.psychologytoday.com/blog/just-listen/201106/do-you-practice-the-golden-rule-take-the-double-standard-assessment-test*

Putnam, M. "Reflections on the Golden Rule". http://www.globalethicsuniversity.com/articles/thegoldenrule.htm

Chapter 7: Make Money Work for You—Not the Other Way Around

The love of money is the root of all evil 1 Timothy 6:10

Money is necessary but not a sufficient condition for the good life, for happiness and wisdom.
Too often we equate having money or making money with being successful and hence happy. We are mystified by those who have no money and yet seem happy and satisfied with their lives.

As David Geller, author of *Wealth & Happiness* notes: "We equate money with security and freedom, which inevitably leaves us feeling insecure and constricted." In his book he shares the theme: Money is not security or freedom. It's not going to turn an unhappy life into a happy one. However, he points out, money is a tool. You can use it as a tool to find happiness and, with it, a better your life.

This same thought is echoed by Charles Richards, author of *The psychology of wealth.* Richards says, "It's no coincidence that money is also called currency, taken from the word CURRENT—the flow of electric charge through a conductor." He goes on to say, "Learning to manage money responsibly and serve others is like being able to use electric current in a productive manner. We can become powerful transformers for the currency of society. How we use that power is a great responsibility."

Research has shown that, beyond having enough money for the necessities of life: food and shelter, there is no proof that having more money makes one happier. Those with a modest income seem as happy—or happier—than those with wealth.

I cannot count how many people I have read about, who won the lottery, but later regretted ever winning it, because to them, it brought them more sorrow than joy.

Whether you love your life or hate it seems largely dependent upon how you use your money. Yes. There is that Golden Rule again. Do you use it to lead a better healthier life, or do you see life enjoyment as sleeping with various women, partying, drugs, etc? Do you use your money to help people and make them happy or do you use it to put people into bondage, reminding them how helpless they are and how low their bank accounts are?

In Matthew 6:19 Jesus taught us "Do not lay up for yourselves treasures on earth." He wasn't saying money itself was bad. Rather he was telling us that hoarding or stockpiling money selfishly was bad.

The Bible didn't tell us money is the root of all evil. It tells us that the *love of money* is the root of all evil.

Geller cautions that trading our content with the life we presently have for a more luxurious lifestyle with lots of things won't make us any happier. Look at the people who won lotteries and became overnight millionaires. Check with them a year or two later and many of them will tell you they wish they'd never won.

Jesus did not ask us to take a vow of poverty. He did not say poverty is some great virtue. Once He told a rich young ruler to sell his possessions and give to the poor. That's because the man was obsessed with his possessions. In Matthew 19:21, the Bible says that he went away sorrowful. Jesus was testing him to see whether God was more important to him than his possessions.

Geller suggests that people should use their money to build better relationships. Money can enhance the lives of the people we care about. Look upon wealth as a resource to build the kind of life we really want. Look at money as a current in your hand for good, not for evil.

How to Make Money Work for You

Strategy #1: Take Stock

What you enjoy most about your life?

What stresses you out?

What parts of your life need positive transformation?

Strategy #2: Examine Your Values about Money

In her book, *The Soul of Money*, author Lynne Twist points out that, by examining our attitudes toward money: how we earn it. How we spend it. To whom, why and how we give it away, we gain insight into our lives, our values, and the *essence* of prosperity.

She explores the extraordinary power money wields over our lives. She also looks at the destructive influence money can have on our self-image and on our relationships with others.

Strategy #3: Share your Goals

Share your goals with friends and family. Choose those who are supportive of your dreams. If friends or family are tepid or unsupportive of your goals and your need for their support, cut them adrift. Do not let them interfere with or dissuade you from your path. Seek out others who will support you. What I mean here is that you simply avoid that particular discussion. Talk about other things. There are so many things to discuss with family and still enjoy family relationships.

Strategy #4: Create an Action Plan

Create an action plan. Decide what needs to change first. Make an outline of your step-by-step plan for reaching your goals. Check off each step as you achieve it and celebrate your progress. Nobody will change your life for the better without your consent, and in many actual cases, nobody will even think about changing your life if you do not ask for it.

Strategy #5: Make Your First Move:

Take baby steps. Your focus is on movement toward a better, and happier, future. Don't bite off too much at once but make a move. The first move is the scariest. Once you've taken it you have proven to yourself and others that you are on your way to achieving your goal.

Strategy #6: Invest in yourself.

As Geller points out: "Success does not require a great deal of money." In fact, Richards notes that you need mostly to have a belief in yourself. In order to move toward a successful, rewarding life, we need to have the willingness to make investment in ourselves. What do you need to reach your goal? Perhaps it is to enroll in college or take a course or attend a conference, rent an office, a computer, materials to create a product you intend to sell, or buy a new "office" wardrobe. Whatever it is: This is an investment in your goal and should not be considered unnecessary, too expensive, a frivolity or something that "can wait until later". Another aspect of self-investment I would like to talk about is spending money to read books on the areas you need improvements in your life.

Some people are tempted to ask me where I got my Master's in Business Administration, when the answer is that my master's degree was in nursing science. I read and studied so much about business management, that I started consulting services for new entrepreneurs. Spend time to read books on the areas you need improvement on. Do not just read to attain degrees. Read to invest in yourself. The money you spend to attend seminars and the money you spend on educational materials are called 'self-development expenses' and are priorities. I read a quote that says that it is only a fool that continues to do the same thing and expects a different result. If you are expecting something different with your life, invest in yourself.

Strategy #7 Figure out What Money CAN Buy

"Money can't buy me love," the Beatles once sang. But can greenbacks buy a measure of happiness? The answer is yes. However, the money needs to be invested in helping you achieve your goal. Money in itself will not buy you happiness. But it is the currency through which you can reach your goal and achieve your dreams.

Strategy #8: Act on your passions

Success and happiness comes from making the right choices and acting on your passions. If your passion is to be a writer, or a dancer, or a teacher, or a doctor, or an artist or a truck driver, then the pursuit of that passion will help you achieve success in your life. I believe that real happiness is doing what you love and getting paid for it. I have always wanted to motivate people. I always gave me inner peace to see someone achieve what they otherwise, would not have if I had not stepped in. When I discovered I could have a career as a motivational speaker and a motivational author, I was extremely glad. This was what I had been doing and derived satisfaction, if I could be paid for it, why not? So my motivational speaking career was lunched. Please visit my website: www.janejohn-nwankwo.com , www.janejohn-nwankwo.org

…And invite me to speak to your audience

Strategy #9: Don't Squander

"Money is an opportunity for happiness," points out University of British Columbia Professor, Dr. Elizabeth

Dunn. She claims people often waste this opportunity. The things they are certain will make them happy often turn out to be disappointments.

The people who won the lottery and ended up broke, unhappy, and bitter months later, squandered their money. Perhaps this happened because it landed in their lap and they had no plan for how they could use it to achieve their goals. They may not even have had clear goals.

Strategy #10: Aim for Long-Term Gains

Have you ever noticed that, in the flurry of buying new things, you are in a euphoric state of pleasure but, once the spree is over you hit a slump? University of California, Riverside professor and author, Sonia Lyubomirsky, refers to this as a brief spike of delight. She notes that the pleasure often vanishes faster than people expect: "like a springtime puddle evaporates under a stifling summer sun."

In order to find happiness, she suggests aiming for long term goals—your action plan—rather than succumbing to brief high points with little coherence to your game plan.

Strategy #11: Use Your Resources to Buy Experiences, not Objects

In a recent Cornell University study, researchers discovered that purchasing an experience improved the subjects' sense of well-being while buying objects resulted in only short-term happiness. Things are temporary. Memories last forever. Instead of always buying a new clothe, why not use some of that money to attend some conferences, short vacations, etc.? Those experiences will last longer.

Strategy #12: Spend on Others

A few years ago, Dr. Elizabeth Dunn conducted an experiment to see how spending money on others affected people. Researchers at the University of British Columbia campus randomly handed students a $5 or $20 bill. Some students were told to spend the money on themselves. Others were told to spend it on other people. They had a day to do so. Those who had been told to spend on others reported feeling happier regardless of the amount.

A University of Oregon study discovered that the emotional rewards of spending on others show up in MRI scans.

Volunteering to give money activated areas of the brain not affected by mandatory giving or forced donations.

Dr. Dunn notes that people are highly social creatures. Thus, much of our happiness hinges on the quality of our interactions with people whether we know them or not. Whatever we do to improve our social connections makes us feel happier.

Strategy #13: Face Reality

We live in a consumer society that glorifies the win, the pitch, the sale. As a society, we have an insatiable appetite for more money, more things. We use money as a measure of self-worth. In *the soul of money*, author Lynne Twist asks us to step back, to look closely at our relationship with people and with money. She asks us to assess our connection to human values, and to change our interpersonal relationship and thus move toward a happier more successful life.

Strategy #14: Find Balance

Too much of anything—money, fame, success, partying, travel… makes us "drunk with excess". Even surfers and shopaholics can reach overload.

We need to approach life with balance. The unhappy winners of boatloads of money discovered all too quickly that there is such a thing as "too much money". Money should be the means by which we direct our energies to achieving our goals—not the goal itself.

Helpful Resources

Dunn, E. "Spend Your Way to Happiness". http://www.thelavinagency.com/blog-spend-your-way-to-happiness-dr-elizabeth-dunn-dan-gilbert-rotman.html

Geller, D. (2012) Wealth & Happiness: Using Your Wealth to Create a Better Life. http://www.amazon.com/Wealth-Happiness-David-Geller-ebook/dp/B0073I4IOG

Kam, K. "Money and Happiness: 5 Ways Your Spending Style Matters" http://www.webmd.com/balance/features/can-money-buy-happiness

Kinder, G. (2000) The Seven Stages of Money Maturity: Understanding the Spirit and Value of Money in Your Life. http://www.amazon.com/Seven-Stages-Money-Maturity-Understanding/dp/0440508339/ref=pd_sim_14_4?ie=UTF8&refRID=1JYG4MNGV26CBGPWC2Q0

Lyubomirsky, S. (2008). *The How of Happiness: A Scientific Approach to Getting the Life You Want.* *http://www.amazon.ca/The-How-Happiness-Approach-Getting/dp/0143114956*

Murphy Casserly, J. (2008). The Emotion Behind Money: Building Wealth from the Inside Out. http://www.amazon.com/The-Emotion-Behind-Money-Building/dp/0980113385/ref=pd_rhf_dp_s_cp_2?ie=UTF8&refRID=1CXXWKZNGWKHGT5EX2MK

Richards, C. (2012) The Psychology of Wealth. http://www.amazon.com/The-Psychology-Wealth-Understand-Relationship/dp/0071789294

Twist, L. (2000) The Soul of Money: Reclaiming the Wealth of Our Inner Resources. http://www.amazon.com/The-Soul-Money-Reclaiming-Resources/dp/039332950X/ref=pd_sim_14_4?ie=UTF8&refRID=1DFRT2Q1S1EYR6KD51EK

Chapter Eight:
Be Accountable: A Responsible Human Being

Work on yourself first. Take responsibility for your own progress

~I Ching

What Does Behaving Responsibly Mean?

Though everyone dreams of riding into the sunset in a convertible and throwing caution in the wind, you can only be James Dean for so long. The truth is that behaving responsibly adds meaning to our lives and allows us to develop character, forge meaningful relationships, and get ahead in the work world. Remember that pet turtle who died because you forgot to feed him? Let's not let that happen again. If you want to learn how to be responsible, just follow along.

Why Do People Avoid Responsibility?

It's tempting to blame everyone around you for your troubles. Pointing your finger at co-workers and claiming you have nothing to do with poor outcomes? Yes, that's the easy part. But I want to let you in on a little secret –the more rewarding path in life comes from a place of personal accountability, not blame. How can this be?

Personal accountability is the belief that you are fully responsible for your own actions and their consequences. It's a choice, a mindset and an expression of integrity. Some individuals exhibit it more than others, but it can and should be learned as it is not only the foundation for a successful personal/professional life, but also a prerequisite for happiness.

You see, your challenges in life are real and will always exist. It's highly doubtful that life will go your way 100% of the time. However, that doesn't mean that these challenges should turn into excuses. Once we stop focusing on what's happening "to" us and focus instead on what we can do within our current circumstances to succeed, we will get the results we're looking for. These results will lead to a happier, more engaged attitude –particularly at work. It reaffirms that you are the architect of your life and that you can handle whatever life tosses your way, especially if you believe that you can do all things through Jesus (Phillipians 4:13).

Why Behave Responsibly?

Do you want to be more successful – at work, at home? Do you want to be more relaxed, less anxious and happier? One of the most powerful ways to achieve these is to make a life-changing choice – and that is to simply be accountable!

Some people go through life feeling that they are victims. They never associate their own actions with why they are where they are in life. Instead, they are convinced that they are victims of bad timing, bad luck, unfaithful friends, unreliable family members or employers who are unscrupulous or hate them or favor others or…

They are never responsible or accountable or to blame for any ill fortune that befalls them. Feeling victimized has nothing to do with ability, intelligence, social background or education. Feeling victimized is a state of mind.
In the parable of the seeds, Jesus said, "*You reap what you sow.*"

In *The Little Prince,* the prince tells his visitor: "It's a question of discipline. When you've finished washing and dressing each morning you must tend your planet."

Ambrose Bierce defined responsibility as "a detachable burden easily shifted to the shoulders of God, Fate, Fortune, Luck or one's neighbor." His point is well taken. We can spend our lives making excuses for why we didn't achieve our goals. We can choose to blame luck, others, or the weather for why we weren't successful. Or we can choose instead to be accountable and take responsibility for our circumstances.

What's involved with Personal Accountability?

1.Being Committed

Being committed means you are willing to do what it takes to get results, no matter what the challenge or task at hand. It means buying in readily to what is asked of you, even if it isn't in your immediate job description. Those who are accountable are willing to fulfill a larger role for the good of the organization.

Studies show that high school athletes actually do better in school. The commitment to sports helps them develop a responsible daily routine that helps them get things done not just on the playing field but in other areas of their life as well.

When you want something done, ask a busy person, "My mother always advises me". And she is right. Busy people always find time to come through for others because they are committed.

2.Taking Initiative

If you see something that needs to be done, don't wait for somebody else to do it. As Gandhi advises, "Be the change you want to see." Everyone can make a positive difference. Remember the man who was bringing love back to New York one interaction at a time? Taking charge will empower you. This will make a difference to your self-confidence and it will improve other areas of your life too.

Initiative is contagious. When others see you taking action they too will get enthused to take initiative. Initiative is self-promotion. When your teachers, your bosses or your parents see that you are someone who will step up to do something, they will have greater confidence in you and they will give you more responsibility. This will give you greater confidence and increase your initiative. Looking for a job promotion? Take responsibility; do a little more than your boss wants you to do, care deeply about the organization, not just your paycheck.

Bosses promote employees who love the organization and have a great sense of responsibility.

3.Being Reliable

It's part of being a responsible person that other people can depend on. If people never ask you to help with homework after school or to do something extra at work or to give them a ride because they just know you'll let them down, then you aren't being responsible. If you promise to do something, be a person who keeps his word.

Being responsible doesn't mean being a doormat. It's okay to say no if you haven't the time or would be inconvenienced or it would be a hardship or the request is outlandish. But if you agree to help someone then being reliable means you will not let them down.

4.Avoid procrastination

In the first chapter of my book, *It's In Your Hands: 5 Strategies To Achieving Your Life Dreams,* I devoted chapter one to procrastination. If you have a chance, buy that book on amazon.com. Irresponsible persons often delay and waste time avoiding a task. They are the ones who miss meetings, ignore deadlines, don't study for tests and turn in shoddy work because they didn't start soon enough.

Procrastinators cram at the last minute, depriving themselves of sleep and using stimulants to stay awake. Don't be a procrastinator. It irritates those with whom you live and work and play. It is not the sign of someone who has personal accountability. Budget your time. Start the task as soon as it is assigned and give yourself time to finish it well. Procrastinators are habitual latecomers. They don't start out to their destination on time because they think they are in control of the traffic, they don't plan for emergencies; they are uncomfortable when the traffic light is showing red for too long. When they eventually reach their destination, they rush from their car in the parking lot to their destination thinking they will cover the time lost within those few steps. Latecomers arrive their destination and start telling everyone why they were late without even being asked, many a time, the audience is not even interested.

5.Be Resilient

You can prove you have personal accountability by taking ownership for tasks and not folding in a whiny heap when the going gets tough. We all hit snags. Everything in life isn't a breeze. Don't throw a pity party when there's a snag in your plans. Resilient people learn to roll with the punches.

Being personally accountable every time you hit a bump in the road? Are you quick to give up at the first sign of trouble?

Yes, it's a valid feeling, but acting on it could mean you are, how shall we say, less than resilient? Channel your inner tenacity and make an effort to bounce back quickly from setbacks. Push on no matter what and you may realize you are stronger and more capable than you knew.

6.Be Consistent.

Your personal accountability won't amount to a hill of beans if it isn't consistent. People in your family, at work, in your community, and your circle of friends need to find you the same every day. Find a workable routine and don't just hit or miss. For example, don't spend an entire day cleaning your room only to ignore it for days and be right back in the same place again. Don't organize your notebook and fall right back into the bad habits that got it all mixed up in the first place. Be consistent with studying, note taking, filing, report writing…whatever responsibilities you have. Be very consistent in praying to God, that way, your strength is continually renewed. Study shows that most individuals who have sunk into clinical depression did not spend quality time praying. Apart from the fact that God hears your prayer, prayer performs a relief action for you.

Your nerves and your mental state relax knowing that someone else is in charge of your problems. And belive me, He is!

7.Be Helpful

Helping others makes them feel good but also makes you feel good about yourself. Being accountable means looking out for others as well as yourself. Develop a habit of a responsible person. Help out your grandparents, your friends, your colleagues, your community.

8.Take Ownership

Taking ownership means accepting the blame but also the credit for the things you do. View both accomplishments and setbacks as part of the stepping-stones to getting better at whatever you do. With success comes happiness.

9.Be responsible for your possession.

Responsible people look after their own things. That includes your car, your money, your home, and your pets. It means locking valuables in the trunk or a safe or a safety deposit box. It means filing important papers in a safe place. It means protecting your identity.

It means keeping your workspace organized and tidy. Keeping your keys in a place where you can always find them; your sunglasses in a case where you can grab them when you need them.

It means guarding your phone, your tablet, your laptop, your jewelry and your prescription glasses so these never need to be replaced.

10. **Stop Making Excuses!**

Pearl Buck said, "We need to restore the full meaning of that old word 'duty'. It's the other side of rights." We will always have things we cannot control. The things we can control are our responsibility. Irresponsible people shift the blame to those factors not under our control—the weather, economic climate, someone else's behavior, unclear instructions, a supplier's mis-shipment, a clerical error. They use these as excuses. Excuses suggest , "I am not responsible for this because..." In essence you are telling people, "I am not responsible."

Another common excuse is, "If…then I would have…" Nice but not taking responsibility!

The next time you start to make an excuse, catch yourself. Instead, admit *why* you really didn't get that thing done. It's best to admit your real reasons for not doing something.

11. **Admit your mistakes.**

I was just telling my husband few seconds ago that one of the reasons why some people have problems in their marriages is pride. They think that admitting that they have made mistakes will hurt their pride with their partner. They refuse to give themselves permission to change their minds. Have you ever thought of the cost of starting a brand new relationship and studying another human being all over again? Why not swallow your pride, take responsibility and work on your current relationship?

Making mistakes is never fun, but people with personal accountability don't view them as failures. Rather, they view them as teachable moments that will help make them better and more successful in the future. They resist the urge to pin the blame on outside forces and, instead, use what they've learned to open up new options for the future.

Mistakes are not character flaws. They are opportunities to learn. People who take personal responsibility look at the situation as a chance to talk about how this can be avoided next time. Making the most of a mistake as an opportunity to learn and being up front about the mistake is a clear sign of accepting responsibility. Others think highly of you if you take personal accountability for it. You are being responsible when you say, "I really messed up here. I won't do it again."

12. **Avoid Scapegoating and Blaming Others**

You failed the math test because you didn't study, not because your teacher hates you. You cheated on your test because you chose to do so, not because the teacher didn't safeguard the test. You were late because you slept in, not because your mother forgot to wake you. Why is it that you are always late because there was traffic? Have you thought that other people also travel through the same freeway and get to work on time? If there is always traffic on that freeway, then start out early. Of course life isn't fair. There will be flat tires and speeding tickets and detours and accidents that slow traffic. Guess what? Others encounter these too.

You can't spend your life blaming things on your parent, your siblings, your teachers or the dog. As Erica Jong noted, when you quit blaming others there is no one left to blame but yourself.

An extreme way you should avoid is trying to blame yourself for everything. That is not what I am talking about here. Just admit it that sometimes, things go wrong.

13. Accept Constructive Criticism

Jim Rohn said, "You must take personal responsibility. You cannot change the circumstances, the seasons, or the wind, but you can change yourself." If the feedback is indeed constructive, a responsible person owes it to himself to be open to criticism. Acknowledge graciously when someone has given you useful feedback. Used correctly, this criticism can help you improve and be more successful.

Whether it is at home, at work, at school or in your community, when you listen to others—a family member, your teachers, a member of the clergy, a psychiatrist, your boss, your doctor, your personal trainer, or your friends—you learn something. After listening and considering you may decide the "friendly advice" or "professional warning" isn't useful or it is mean spirited or the person giving it has no idea what he is talking about. However, the responsible thing to do is to listen, consider, and use what seems applicable.

It is irresponsible to refuse to listen to helpful suggestions. You need not take them but you owe it to yourself, your family, your employer, your friends, to at least think about it.

Keep in mind that your family, your teachers, your superiors and your friends may have difficulty giving you criticism. It is a risk to the relationship they have with you. Treat it as a gift to you not as a personal insult. You don't have to take it but you can listen and thank the person for his concern.

14. Be a Lifelong Learner

Continuing to learn from every mistake, every success, every new experience, every person you meet is the way to be personally accountable. As Michel Legrand put it, """The more I live, the more I learn. The more I learn, the more I realize, the less I know." That's the thing about lifelong learning and personal accountability: it's a lifetime process. You owe it to yourself to continue to grow and change and learn.

15. **Understand Responsibility is an Earned Privilege**

Joan Didion stated: ‘The willingness to accept responsibility for one’s own life is the source from which self-respect springs.” Responsibility is earned. It's not an entitlement. If you’ve shown no eagerness to take on added responsibility, is it any wonder people don’t see you as responsible? If you’ve been nonchalant about the responsibilities you already have, others won’t feel confident about your taking on extra privileges. You earn responsibility.

You might think, "What I have to do now are so boring or stupid or a lot of bother. Why take on more? Responsible people don’t shirk added challenge. Doing things to the best of your ability is being personally accountable. Everything you do isn’t going to be easy or glorious or mentally challenging. Guess what? Others feel the same way. It’s not fun. Otherwise they wouldn’t call it work!

16. Stop Whining!

Whining is like scapegoating. It only goes to show you are not taking personal accountability.

If you do nothing but complain about everything--your job, the boss, your partner, your debts, your kids, the weather, the clients… you develop a reputation as a Wendy Whiner. Is that how you want to be known?

Complaining is very much like blaming. It is not taking responsibility. It is not being personally accountable. Complaining is blaming the world for your problems. Instead, take the initiative to change situations you do not like.

17. **Stop Playing the Victim.**

The world is not out to get you. If you want to start being responsible, then stop thinking that everyone is out to make you fail or look bad. The police officer didn't give you that speeding ticket to punish you. You were breaking the law and behaving in a manner that was dangerous to yourself and others.

Your boss didn't overlook you for a raise because he hates you. Your performance didn't merit a raise. You didn't get the promotion because someone else had better qualifications or worked harder or had better interview skills.

Stop looking for ways to make yourself and others feel sorry for you and figure out what YOU can do to avoid another speeding ticket, get that raise or secure that promotion.

18. Accept what you cannot Control.

The Alcoholics Anonymous Prayer probably says this best:

GOD, grant me the serenity to accept the things I cannot change,

The Courage to change the things I can,

and the wisdom to know the difference.

Living ONE DAY AT A TIME; Enjoying one moment at a time;

Accepting hardship as the pathway to peace.

Taking, as He did, this sinful world as it is, not as I would have it.

Trusting that He will make all things right if I surrender to His Will;

That I may be reasonably happy in this life, and supremely happy with Him forever in the next.

Just as you need to accept responsibility for your actions, stop scapegoating, blaming others and acting like a victim, you need to recognize that, while there is a time to take the initiative there is also a time when you accept what you cannot change. Be careful that it really is something you cannot change, because it's easy to make that an excuse for not taking responsibility.

Some things are just simply beyond your control. Your best friend's overeating, your mother's smoking, your boss' womanizing are not your responsibility and you can't change them. Focus instead on what you can control. Don't try to fix all of the problems of the world, or you will die and the world will still continue. My father, late Elder John Onwere once told me that the best person to have died for the world was Jesus Christ. "He has already done it, my daughter, so cherish your life".

19. **Practice self-discipline.**

When you practice self-discipline in the way you talk, you eat, you think, and you do it repeatedly, it becomes a habit.

As Jessie Owens observed, “We all have dreams. But in order to make dreams come into reality, it takes an awful lot of determination, dedication, self-discipline, and effort.” Responsible people are accountable for their actions. They don’t drink and drive. They don’t overspeed. They don’t murder and steal. They do not take drugs, smoke or drink to excess. They don’t set fire to people’s houses, abuse their family or their pets. Responsible people practice self-discipline. That eliminates shooting sprees at work, road rage, temper tantrums and running naked through the street. Being responsible doesn't mean you have to have the work ethic of a drone or the mental abilities of a rocket scientist, or the routine of a soldier. It does mean that you know how and when work needs to be done. Self-disciplined people set goals and meet them. Self-disciplined people don’t get distracted or procrastinate.

20. Reward yourself for goals achieved.

When you have achieved a goal or a step on the way to that goal, you owe it to yourself and those who have supported you to celebrate that achievement. The rewards can be as tangible as a new scarf or as intangible as a walk on the beach but they need to be acknowledged.

21. Stay Motivated

There are a number of ways to stay motivated. Some work better for some than others. Find what keeps you motivated and use it. It might be a list you check off, a reward as you complete a task, meditation, guided visualization or a mentor. Whatever keeps you up to the task should be embraced.

LIFE IS FULL OF CHALLENGES. RESPONSIBLE PEOPLE DEAL WITH CHALLENGES WITH A POSITIVE MIND.

22. **Learn to deal with the hard stuff.**

Personal accountability demands that you accept setbacks, disappointments, mistakes and do overs with confidence and grace. Life is full of challenges.

If you want to be responsible, you have to deal with them just as you deal with life's triumphs.

You need to know how to deal with tragedy and hardship. That's when having that support group will be invaluable. As George Bernard Shaw said, "We are made wise not by the recollection of our past, but by the responsibility for our future."

23. **Learn to manage your money.**

In a previous chapter we talked about money management. I mention it again because it is another important part of personal accountability. Responsible persons have budgets and long-range plans. They don't live from paycheck to paycheck, wondering where their money went to. They know exactly where their money goes each month. They defer short-term pleasures for long-term goals. They practice moderation, and avoid impulsivity. As God began to gradually increase our income, I realized that it was very easy to see your money 'fly away' if you do not have good plans in place.

I think the best way to measure if you manage your money well is to ask yourself if you always have emergency money. Do you always have to look outside when there is an emergency money that you didn't plan for but that would really need to be spent?

Another way to measure your money management is to take a stock of how many of your plans that you actually followed through without distractions. These, I think are the top most two ways of measuring your money management. There are other ways, of course.

Useful Resources

Bierce, A. (1911). *The Devil's Dictionary.*

Branden, N. (1997) Taking Responsibility: Self-Reliance and an Accountable Life. http://www.amazon.ca/Taking-Responsibility-Nathaniel-Branden-Ph-D/dp/0684832488

Connors, R. and Smith, T. (2011) How Did that Happen? http://www.amazon.com/How-Did-That-Happen-Accountable/dp/1591844142/ref=pd_bxgy_14_img_z

Evans, H. (2008) Winning with Accountability. http://www.amazon.com/Winning-Accountability-Language-High-Performing-Organizations/dp/0981924204

de Saint-Exupery, A. (1943) *The Little Prince.*

Folkman, J. "The 8 Great Accountability Skills for Business Success". http://www.forbes.com/sites/joefolkman/2014/11/14/how-do-you-score-the-8-great-accountability-skills-for-business-success/

Izzo, J. (2011) Stepping Up: How Taking Responsibility Changes Everything. http://www.amazon.ca/Stepping-Up-Responsibility-Changes-Everything/dp/1609940571

Jong, Erica. (2008) *Fear of Flying.* http://www.amazon.com/Fear-Flying-Erica-Jong/dp/045120994X

Chapter Nine:

Practice Self-Discipline

What is Self-Discipline?

Call it restraint or self-control, self-discipline is what keeps us under control or within limits. These limits might be the law or social mores or fear of being caught or fear of our superiors or conscience.

When you are a teenager this control is often peer pressure or looking like a dork in front of your friends. Younger children often practice self-discipline because they wish to please their parents.

As we grow older we practice self-discipline to satisfy our partners, our bosses, the legal system and the social codes of our culture. Self-discipline is the ability to control impulses, emotions, wants and deeds. Self-discipline means being able to resist immediate pleasure and instant gratification for long-term gain and fulfillment of more meaningful goals.

Self-discipline is staying home to study while your friends go to the beach. Self-discipline is going to work when your friends are taking Friday off to spend a long week-end in Vegas.

When you have self-discipline you can make mature decisions, take wise actions, and execute a well thought out game plan regardless of the temptations, the obstacles, the discomfort, or the difficulties, that may stand in your way.

The Bible has quite a lot to say about self-discipline.

In Hebrews 12:11 it says, "For the moment all discipline seems painful rather than pleasant, but later it yields the peaceful fruit of righteousness to those who have been trained by it."
Proverbs 25:28 state: A man without self-control is like a city broken into and left without walls.

There are actually more than 30 references to self-discipline in the Bible.

Titus 2:11:14 urges us, "For the grace of God has appeared, bringing salvation for all people, training us to renounce ungodliness and worldly passions, and to live self-controlled, upright, and godly lives in the present age, waiting for our blessed hope, the appearing of the glory of our great God and Savior Jesus Christ, who gave himself for us to redeem us from all lawlessness and to purify for himself a people for his own possession who are zealous for good works."

What does Self-Discipline have to do with Success?

Theodore Roosevelt said, "With self-discipline almost anything is possible."

Clint Eastwood points out that self-discipline gives us power. "Respect your efforts, respect yourself. Self-respect leads to self-discipline. When you have both firmly under your belt, that's real power."

The truth is: No personal success, no achievement, no goal, can be achieved without self-discipline. Self- discipline is the trait we most need to succeed. It is more important than insight or intelligence or motivation. To achieve personal excellence, athletic excellence, creativity, ingenuity we must have self-discipline. All the talent in the world will not make you a famous artist, a great inventor, a successful scientist or a prima ballerina if you don't have self-discipline.

How Do You Develop Self-Discipline?

1. **Baby steps**

Change does not take place overnight. Muscles and skills and habits take time to build. So does self-discipline. The more you train your restraint, the stronger it will become. Don't try to do too much too fast. Like exercise, you could overdo it and cause a setback. Proceed cautiously, one step at a time building your self-discipline. Begin with the resolve to go forward. Learn as you go what it takes to get there.

2. Know Your Triggers

What motivates you? What are your bad triggers? Begin by learning about yourself! Urges, temptations, cravings, desires can be very difficult to fight off. Learn what these are. Find out when your resistance is low. Then discover how to avoid those situations.

If you find alcohol or French fries, or gambling or chocolate cake tempting, avoid them. Don't have them around where they can weaken your resolve. That is just common sense. Don't set yourself up for moments of weakness. If you are trying to lose weight and you love ice creams, don't purchase them, store them in your freezer, and believe you will take them with caution; the best thing? don't purchase them at all. If stress is a problem or not getting enough sleep leaves you in a weakened state, then set up an environment that encourages the building of self-discipline rather than one that puts it at risk. Don't self-sabotage. Instead, remove the potential problems. Surround yourself with things and people and situations that soothe and encourage what you want to achieve.

Learn what encourages, energizes and motivates you. Your willpower decreases as your energy declines. Do things that keep your energy up whether that is exercise, being outdoors, surrounding yourself with energetic people or listening to lively music.

Laughter is energizing and motivating. Surround yourself with people, things and situations which make you smile and laugh outright. Enjoy what you are doing. This will make it easier to be self-disciplined. If every day is a drag then you need to get out of that rut and put some joy and fun back into your life. My schedule is so tight, that if I need to get everything done, I don't need to sleep; I don't need to have time for my husband or children; I don't need to have time to read books; I don't even need to have time to relax and watch a movie. So, I thought of how to solve this problem and two things came to my mind: Delegation and Self-discipline.

I need to be able to trust other people to perform those tasks I think only me could perform. I had to train and just supervise. I had to discipline myself to STOP. "It is time to be a mother" I have to tell myself, "It is time to be a wife"; "It is time to be a minister" "It is time for me". Without self-discipline, you cannot have a happy life.

3. Establish a Routine

When you have decided what's important, which goals you are striving for, set up a routine to help you achieve them. If your goal is to eat healthily or lose weight, resolve to eat several servings of fruits and vegetables each day. Set up a routine where you exercise for at least half an hour each day at the same time. Make it part of your daily routine. Make it a part of building self-discipline. If you are on the part of losing weight, I suggest my book : *Weight Loss Inspiration.*

Get rid of bad triggers, those self-defeating habits. These might include eliminating junk food from your cupboards and your shopping list. It may mean taking an extra half hour to walk or bike to work instead of starting the car. It may mean carrying a healthy lunch and good mid-morning and mid-afternoon snacks to work instead of going out for lunch or hitting the vending machines when the munchies hit. It may mean you go for a walk or to the gym at lunch instead of sitting with colleagues. Attitude is half the battle. Plan to achieve your goal and set up an environment that is helpful to keeping your resolution. Routines once established will become so automatic you will pack that healthy lunch, walk to work, exercise and avoid vending machines without even giving it a second thought!

4. Practice Self-Denial

Learn to say no to cravings, feelings, impulses, desires, and urges. Self-discipline involves doing what you know is right, even if you don't feel like doing it. It is having water even when you'd like wine. It is skipping dessert and having a piece of fruit instead. It is limiting TV watching or computer time and instead doing something active like going for a bike ride.

Self-discipline means resist the urge to yell at that other driver who just cut you off or your kid who has just broken a window or a colleague who missed an important deadline. Self-restraint means you stop and think. Count to ten before you react to an irritating situation. Self-control means you give yourself time to think about consequences of your actions or words before you say or do something. Practicing self-restraint, it helps you develop a habit of keeping other things under control. Sometimes, I have said things and quickly ask myself "Did I just say that?", I learn from it and try to improve when similar situations arise. Self-discipline is a continuous process.

5. Get Involved

Remember the Participation ads? Sports—or any activity for that matter—can enhance your self-discipline. Getting involved encourages you to set goals, focus your thoughts and emotions on learning more, helping others, getting more physically fit, or completing a project. Participating in sports or hobbies or pastimes provides an opportunity to learn, to work hard, to strive to do your best. Getting involved means focusing your organizational skills, your skills, your talents, your energy on reaching a goal. This self-disciplines carries over into the rest of your life.

Learning to do anything from volleyball to tap dancing to playing a musical instrument, or baking a pie can be great practice for self-discipline. Focus, learning, repetition, and execution are invaluable opportunities to exercise self-discipline.

Achieving self-discipline in any area of your life builds confidence in your ability to practice self-control. Restraint and application become habits.

6. **Seek models of self-discipline**

Whether it is people you've read about like Gandhi or people in your community whose self-control you admire, these people can help you build your self-discipline by their own examples. Michael Jordan insists his greatness as a basketball player came more from his hard work, repetitions, self-discipline than it did from talent. Lots of people are talented hockey players but few become a Wayne Gretzky. Few achieve the musical fame of Yo-Yo Ma athough they may have as much natural ability. Beyond skill you have to have the will to practice, practice, practice while others are out having fun. Perfecting your craft like the William sisters takes hundreds of hours of tennis play every week. That takes self-discipline. It also helps you resolve to have encouraging parents, coaches, siblings, friends and partners.

7. **See your Successes**

To be successful you have to be able to see yourself succeeding. You have to visualize yourself reaching your goals. High achievers in every field can see themselves in that winner's circle, accepting that award, finding a cure for cancer.

Achieving success is a three-step process that begins with imagining yourself reaching your goal.

Photo courtesy of Pinterest

When you believe you can achieve your goal, when you can feel how rewarding it will be, it increases your impetus and builds the self-discipline necessary for reaching that goal.

Imagination has helped me a great deal in achieving my goals. I imagine how things will be when it happens.

What are the Rewards?

No one said self-discipline was easy or fun. Others who lack self-discipline are out there like the grasshopper fiddling the summer away while you, the proverbial ant store up food for winter.

But there are rewards. With every goal reached you gain greater self-confidence. This, in turn, gives you the motivation and impetus to strive for the next goal, even more certain that you will be able to achieve it.

When you practice self-discipline you accomplish more. You are more productive and hence more successful at achieving your goals.

When you have self-discipline you have a greater tolerance for stress, frustration, obstacles, disappointments and setbacks. You are able to put these all in perspective because you are resilient and because you have a clear goal in mind. Self-discipline helps you achieve better health, healthier finances, good work habits, and improved interpersonal relationships.

When you have self-discipline you can handle those difficult goals confidently, consistently, and efficiently. The more self-disciplined you become, the more others look up to you, admire and want to emulate you. You become a model, a mentor, an inspiration for others.

In Galatians 5:23 the Bible advises: "Gentleness, self-control; against such things there is no law." With self-discipline you can accomplish just about anything you set your mind to.

Useful Resources

Baumeister, R. (2012) *Willpower: Rediscovering the Greatest Human Strength.* http://www.amazon.ca/Willpower-Rediscovering-Greatest-Human-Strength/dp/0143122231

Duhigg, W. (2014) *The Power of Habit: Why We Do what We Do in Life and in Business.* http://www.amazon.ca/gp/product/0385669763/ref=pd_lpo_sbs_dp_ss_2?pf_rd_p=1977604502&pf_rd_s=lpo-top-stripe&pf_rd_t=201&pf_rd_i=0143122231&pf_rd_m=A3DWYIK6Y9EEQB&pf_rd_r=0X36V4PH92YAVGDMWA58

Hardy, D. (2012) *The Compound Effect. Jump Start Your Income, Your Life, Your Success.* http://www.amazon.ca/The-Compound-Effect-Darren-Hardy/dp/159315724X/ref=pd_sim_14_7?ie=UTF8&refRID=15SN9BT9QFSQ24CKS8Q4

McGonigal,K. (2013) *The Willpower Instinct.* http://www.amazon.ca/gp/product/1583335080/ref=pd_lpo_sbs_dp_ss_1?pf_rd_p=1977604502&pf_rd_s=lpo-top-stripe&pf_rd_t=201&pf_rd_i=0143122231&pf_rd_m=A3DWYIK6Y9EEQB&pf_rd_r=0X36V4PH92YAVGDMWA58

Steenbarger, B. (2003) *A Trader's Guide to Self-Discipline.* https://www.chapters.indigo.ca/en-ca/books/product/9781592800926-item.html?mkwid=sP8ld10FR_dc&pcrid=44154474422&pkw=&pmt=&s_campaign=goo-Shopping_Books&gclid=CjwKEAjw3PGtBRCWgajpu_uY9hYSJAAICRal_KqvvsPdmgZ0byomjL6tWVbNLVrH42wfHDok_OldmhoCaB_w_wcB

Pink, D. (2011) *Drive: The Surprising Truth about what Motivates Us.* http://www.amazon.ca/Drive-Surprising-Truth-About-Motivates/dp/1594484805/ref=pd_sim_14_2?ie=UTF8&refRID=1ZSAVCH0F2EBJR96ZWXY

Tracy, B. (2011) *No Excuses! The Power of Self-Discipline.* http://www.amazon.ca/No-Excuses-The-Power-Self-Discipline/dp/1593156324

Epilogue

Whether or not we are successful in life has a lot to do with how we define success. And how we define success has a lot to do with our belief system. It is interesting to see how famous people whom society would call "successful" look at the concept of success.

In her book, Thrive, founder of *Huffington Post,* Arianna Huffington writes, that our society uses power and money as parameters for success. She adds: "To live the lives we truly want and deserve, and not just the lives we settle for, we need a Third Metric…a third measure of success that goes beyond the two metrics of money and power, and consists of four pillars: well-being, wisdom, wonder, and giving."

Legendary Basketball coach John Wooden defines success : "Success is peace of mind, which is a direct result of self-satisfaction in knowing you did your best to become the best you are capable of becoming."

Renowned poetess Maya Angelou defines success as, "liking yourself, liking what you do, and liking how you do it."

However we choose to define success, it is important that we feel fulfilled by what we are doing and we leave the world a better place for our having been here. For me, Stephen Grellet's words resound:

"I shall pass through this world but once.

Any good therefore that I can do or any kindness that I can show to any human being,

let me do it now.

Let me not defer or neglect it,

for I shall not pass this way again."

Whenever you are tempted to overwhelmed with life struggles, take a deep breath, remember the principles you have learned and DON'T WORRY, BE HAPPY!

ABOUT THE AUTHOR

Jane John-Nwankwo CPT, DSD, RN, MSN, PHN is a motivational speaker and published author of more than 50 books which include textbooks for healthcare training, fiction for entertainment, and motivational books.
Simply search "Books by Jane John-Nwankwo"
On Amazon.com

Visit her websites:

www.janejohn-nwankwo.com

www.djngbooks.com

www.janejohn-nwankwo.org

Book Jane John-Nwankwo as your motivational speaker now at www.JaneJohn-Nwankwo.com

With more than 10 years as a professional speaker, Jane John-Nwankwo can hold any audience sitting straight on their chairs for any length of time! She is a seminar leader and a published author of more than 50 books including textbooks for healthcare training, fiction for entertainment, books for new entrepreneurs and motivational and inspirational books like the "It's in your hands" series.

She received her Masters of Science in Nursing from University of Phoenix, and has attained other professional certifications and awards. She is a successful entrepreneur of a couple of businesses including educational institutions, a healthcare staffing agency and consulting firms. Her speaking interests include: Motivational speeches for new business owners, Motivational speeches for any category of people, Employee seminars, Students' Empowerment, Healthcare topics, Topics related to women and any Christian topic. Book a speaking appointment today and become a repeat customer because of 100% satisfaction.

www.janejohn-nwankwo.com

Made in the USA
Columbia, SC
28 September 2024

42857623R00109